In This Place...

Ruth Fromstein

Bloomington, IN Milton Keynes, UK
authorHOUSE®

AuthorHouse™
1663 Liberty Drive, Suite 200
Bloomington, IN 47403
www.authorhouse.com
Phone: 1-800-839-8640

AuthorHouse™ UK Ltd.
500 Avebury Boulevard
Central Milton Keynes, MK9 2BE
www.authorhouse.co.uk
Phone: 08001974150

First published by AuthorHouse 11/13/2006

ISBN: 978-1-4259-7487-9 (sc)

Printed in the United States of America
Bloomington, Indiana

This book is printed on acid-free paper.

Dedication

To Lillian Friedman

She loved the temple with all her heart and soul, and she made an indelible imprint on it.

She knew its history, its rabbis, its families.

She guarded its records and assembled a treasure trove of photographs, letters, documents and memorabilia.

Her work was the foundation on which this history was built.

In This Place...*

...In this place we find God

...In this place we find our way in the world

...In this place we draw near to our people Israel

...In this place we bind to all people

...In this place we be drawn to the Torah

...In this place we learn

Rabbi David Polish

1985

* It is in Congregation Emanu-El B'ne Jeshurun that 150 years of Milwaukee families have learned what it means to be Jewish. May we remember the visions which entered the hearts of the people, the cause to which they dedicated themselves, the burdens which they bore with gladness.

Milwaukee in the 1850's was a very different city from Milwaukee in the 21st century. Paved streets were non-existent. Horse-drawn carriages, fire pumpers, trolleys and beer wagons clattered over mud or gravel roads. Watering troughs for horses were a common sight.

Since it would be decades before electric lighting, there could be none of the traffic lights and neon signs that fill the streets today. The railroads had not yet come to Milwaukee and ships on the Lake Michigan route were the only long distance carriers of goods and people.

Familiar landmarks today known as symbolic of Old Milwaukee would not appear for another 45 to 50 years. There was no City Hall, no Pfister Hotel, no Pabst Theater, no Water Tower rising high above Lake Michigan. A synagogue was nowhere to be found.

Barely out of the pioneer fur trading days of Solomon Juneau, Milwaukee had been incorporated officially as a city in 1846, just two years before Wisconsin statehood.

Twelve to Begin With

By the 1850's immigrants from Europe, arriving daily by lake steamer, traveled to inns and hotels via hackney coaches. Unrest and revolution in the German states in 1848 impelled thousands of people to leave their homeland. Already home to a German-speaking community, Milwaukee became a magnet for the immigrants. Among them were three separate groups of families who founded the Jewish community and formed the predecessors to the present day Congregation Emanu-El B'ne Jeshurun.

In the autumn of 1847, barely one year after Milwaukee's incorporation, 12 men gathered on Yom Kippur at the home of Isaac Neustadel for the city's first Jewish religious service. They later formed an organization and purchased a one-acre plot of ground in the Ninth Ward to serve as a Jewish cemetery. Officers of the fledgling cemetery association were president Gabriel Schoyer, believed to be the city's first Jewish settler, and secretary Solomon Adler, one of the founders of David Adler & Sons, a pioneer clothing company.

The cemetery, located on Hopkins St. became the burial ground of Temple Imanu-Al and the first funeral was conducted there one year later. The last burial on the small tract was in 1888.

Yom Kippur of 1848 found the same group observing the Holy Day at the home of Henry Neuhaus. A year later, they held Day of Atonement services in a rented room above Nathan Pereles' grocery store on the corner of Third and Chestnut Sts. (now Juneau Ave.).

For 150 years, the Jewish worship community has been characterized by dissention and disagreement over liturgical practices, over rabbis, over synagogue location and perhaps a myriad of other spats. The saga of congregational history is replete with one disagreement after another, often spawning a new congregation that sometimes long outlived the reason it was formed

During 1850, and in its fourth year of ad hoc services, the organization formally became Congregation Imanu-Al, which held regular worship services above the Pereles store. Formed in the German tradition, Imanu-Al soon encountered resistance from a significant group advocating the Polish tradition. In 1854, they left to form a second congregation, Ahavath Emuno, which met in the old Washington Hall on Oneida St. (now E. Wells St.).

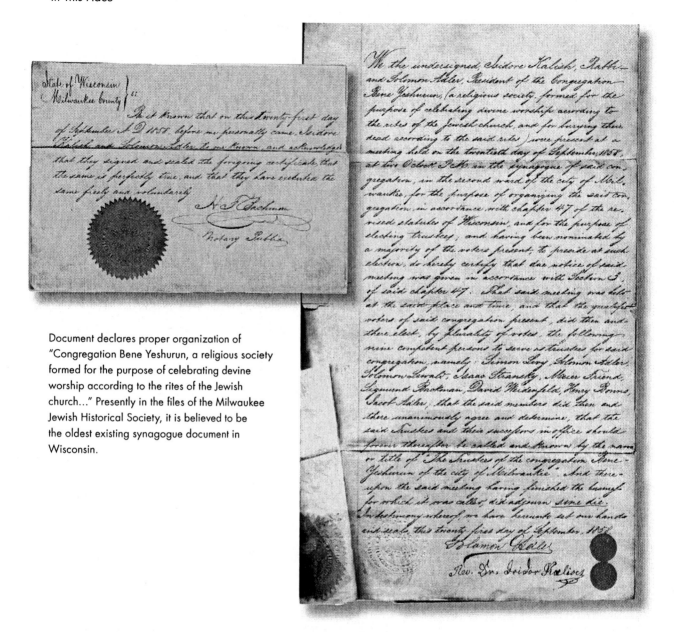

Document declares proper organization of "Congregation Bene Yeshurun, a religious society formed for the purpose of celebrating devine worship according to the rites of the Jewish church..." Presently in the files of the Milwaukee Jewish Historical Society, it is believed to be the oldest existing synagogue document in Wisconsin.

Community peace could not obtain for long however, and Ahavath Emuno members who preferred the German style seceded not to the original Imanu-Al, but to organize a third congregation, Anshe Emeth. All of the early immigrants brought their Orthodox practices with them to these new congregations, which operated with largely Orthodox customs.

By 1856, however, Reform Judaism developed in
America and its founder, Isaac Mayer Wise paid Milwaukee
a visit that August. He was distressed to find 200 local
Jewish families divided into three synagogues. Devoting his
two sermons to community unity, he was able to persuade
Imanu-Al and Ahavath Emuno to join together in their
German, now Reform, style, resulting in the establishment
of B'ne Jeshurun in 1856. It was another three years before
the third congregation, Anshe Emeth, in the throes of a
new building project, would abandon that plan and agree
to merge with B'ne Jeshurun, where the cornerstone of a
new structure had already been laid. For the first time,
Milwaukee Jews were united in one congregation of 115

Beginning the process of
gradual reform at Emanu-
El, Rabbi Moritz Spitz
instituted Confirmation as
a culmination to religious
school studies. His first
class in 1875 consisted of
six girls and two boys.

Rabbi Isidor Kalisch

families. It's building would be located at 4th St. between
State and Prairie (now Highland Ave.). Nathan Pereles,
Milwaukee's first lawyer, was elected president.

The growing congregation soon advertised for its first
rabbi in the American Israelite, a newspaper edited by Isaac
Mayer Wise. Rabbi Wise again traveled from Cincinnati to
attend dedication services for the new building.

The first rabbi, Isidor Kalisch, born in Posen, Prussia
in 1816, gradually introduced more liberal practices. He
instituted the first Confirmation service and began mixed
seating of men and women. Sermons were conducted in
German, still the native language of most members. Before
the merger into B'ne Jeshurun, rabbis had customarily

Rabbi Ferdinand Leopold Sarner

Rabbi Samson Falk

performed the functions of cantor, teacher and *shochet* in
addition to their rabbinic duties. It was during the tenure of
Rabbi Kalisch that the first cantor was hired.

As the Civil War emerged, Rabbi Kalisch petitioned for
the appointment of Jewish chaplains for the Union soldiers.
He protested an act of congress that required chaplains to
be "ministers of a Christian denomination". As a result of
his efforts, that act was amended and President Lincoln
subsequently appointed Jewish chaplains for the first time in
American history.

When Rabbi Kalisch departed the city, he was replaced
briefly in 1860 by Rabbi Ferdinand Leopold Sarner, but
for the three succeeding years, the congregation functioned

Rabbi G.M. Cohen

Ark from B'ne Jeshurun's downtown temple built in 1886. The ark was preserved when the structure was destroyed. It remained in an upstairs chapel in the Kenwood Emanu-El until it was donated to the restoration of the Civil War vintage Synagogue Shaare Shemaim in Madison, WI. in 1972. The historic building is in Madison's James Madison Park. When the ark was disassembled for transport, old wood panels and carvings of pine and cherry emerged from the black walnut exterior and were believed to be woods from B'ne Jeshurun's original ark from the 4th and State Sts. temple built in 1857.

without a rabbi or cantor until the 1863 arrival of Rabbi Samson Falk, whose tenure lasted through the Civil War period. President Andrew Johnson had designated June 1, 1865 as a National Day of Mourning after the recent assassination of President Abraham Lincoln. Rabbi Falk honored the occasion with a sermon dealing with the life of Lincoln.

The stay of his successor, Rabbi G.M. Cohen, was also very brief. He was followed by Rabbi Elias Eppstein, who served B'ne Jeshurun for 11 years from 1869 to 1880. His

Saturday morning sermons were preached in German and regular Sunday lectures were in English. He founded a Juvenile Society for students in the synagogue's school. The program was a forerunner of the Junior Congregation, which provided a popular weekly educational and social evening for teenagers in the 1930's, 40's and 50's.

While in Milwaukee, Rabbi Eppstein conducted a survey of local Jewry. His census counted a total local Jewish population of 2,074. At the time of his arrival, the congregation was already leaving most of its Orthodox practices behind. During his tenure, a lively community began to seek further changes in religious practice. Many dissatisfied members wanted to progress more rapidly

Rabbi Elias Eppstein

Rabbi Emanuel Gerechter

toward Reform. In addition, increasing membership required expanded facilities, but leaders could not decide whether to build anew or enlarge its 4th St. building. A further controversy pitted members satisfied with their West Side synagogue against others who wanted a more favorable East Side location, a quandary that would be revisited in future years. Soon the East Side proponents left B'ne Jeshurun to form a new congregation, Emanu-El.

After the departure of the 35 dissidents, Rabbi Eppstein remained in B'ne Jeshurun's pulpit for another decade. He was followed by Rabbi Emanuel Gerechter, who arrived from synagogues in Detroit and Grand Rapids, Michigan. During his time the congregation engaged a cantor and organist and formed a

This stately structure housed Congregation B'ne Jeshurun from 1886 at 10th & Cedar Sts. until the merger with Emanu-El. The Cedar St. property is now the site of Milwaukee County Courthouse, where a plaque today commemorates this site of the city's first synagogue building.

Rabbi Victor Caro

choir. Rabbi Gerechter spent 12 years in his position from 1880 to 1892 and later headed a synagogue in Appleton, Wisconsin.

He was succeeded by the dynamic Rabbi Victor Caro, who was born in Budapest, educated in a Polish yeshiva and ordained in Berlin by a "modern" Orthodox institution. He emigrated to the United States in 1881 and held two American pulpits before coming to Milwaukee. A man with very strong views, Rabbi Caro spoke out against ostentatious living and showy funerals of his increasingly prosperous congregants. He opposed Jewish separatism,

Rabbi Charles S. Levi

denouncing parochial schools and emerging Hebrew trade unions. Although against Zionism, his position was not strong. That he knew he was controversial is indicated by his statement to the congregation:

> "I know I have not pleased many of you because
> I have spoken often in forcible and bold language.
> I have done so because I will be held responsible at
> the bar of justice."

Despite his forcible manner, he was well-loved by his members and was known as a tireless worker both at B'ne Jeshurun and in the community. Rabbi Caro served for two decades, carrying the congregation into the 20th century before giving way in 1912 to Rabbi Charles S. Levi.

Rabbi Levi stood firmly for Reform Judiasm and his
services were almost like those of his contemporaries,
Emanu-El's Rabbis Samuel Hirshberg and Joseph Baron.
Although very closely akin to Emanu-El, whose new
structure on Kenwood Blvd. was completed in 1923 and
appeared large enough to house the combined groups, Rabbi
Levi opposed merger, perhaps because he saw little future
for himself when Emanu-El was already staffed with two
very able rabbis, Hirshberg and Baron. The announcement
of his retirement was the final impetus for the merger and
in 1927 they combined to become Congregation Emanu-
El B'ne Jeshurun housed in the new building at 2419 E.
Kenwood Blvd.

From Dissidence to Strength

It was 1869 when the 35 dissident members left B'ne Jeshurun to form the Reform Congregation Emanu-El, at first holding services in Field's Hall, rented for $400 a year. Two years later, they broke ground and laid the cornerstone for a synagogue structure on the East Side at

14

Left: Exterior of the 1872 home of Emanu-El. A lovely building, but without central heating for its first nine years. Electricity was not added until a remodeling after 11 years.

Right: Interior of the first Temple Emanu-El building constructed in 1872 at Broadway & Martin (now State) Sts. at a cost of approximately $60,000.

Martin and Main Sts. (now Broadway and State Sts.). The cornerstone was celebrated by a municipal parade with state and city officials attending.

The dedication held August 31, 1872 was on land that cost $7,000 and a building costing $60,000 of which only $14,000 was mortgage debt payable in five years. But congregants worshipped for nine years in the building without central heating. Electricity was not added for an additional 11 years and the structure was finally remodeled in 1896, remaining its home until the final Sabbath service on March 22, 1923. The following Sabbath was celebrated in the new Kenwood Blvd. facility. A new era for a powerful new Congregation Emanu-El B'ne Jeshurun in a stately new synagogue had begun.

David Adler, founder and president of Imanu Al, later
president of B'ne Jeshurun and five times leader of Emanu-El.

David Adler, the first president, had earlier served as
president of B'ne Jeshurun. After his first Emanu-El term
he was later reelected on five different occasions totaling
18 years of leadership service in these early years.

The years following the split from B'ne Jeshurun
were busy ones. Members had voted to pattern their
sanctuary after the stately, Temple Emanu-El on New
York's fashionable Fifth Ave. and the religious home of the
Guggenheims, Warburgs, Frankfurters and other prominent
Jewish immigrant families of the 19th century.

In 1874, the congregation became one of the first in
the nation to join the recently formed Union of American

Hebrew Congregations (now Union for Reform Judaism). Although all of the founders were native-speaking Germans, they decided immediately that all business should be conducted in English. Soon they purchased a 10-acre parcel of land near Forest Home Cemetery for $3,000, a plot later named Greenwood Cemetery. The Emanu-El Ladies Society was instrumental in raising the money for Emanu-El Hall, an addition adjacent to the synagogue to be used for meetings and various celebrations.

Emanu-El held two services each Saturday morning— one traditional, the other with "covered heads". Rabbi Moritz Spitz, who would serve 1872 to 1878 asked to

Early Confirmation classes were small, personal experiences. This Emanu-El class with Rabbi Spitz (circa 1875) consisted of just five confirmands.

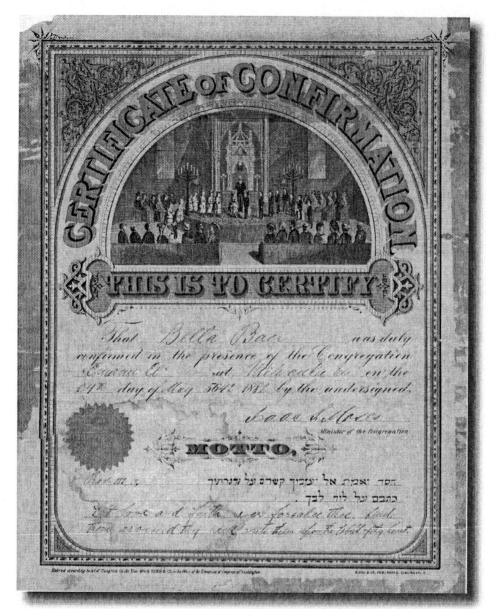

First started in 1875, Confirmation has always been an important event as evidenced by this elaborate certificate, which was awarded at Emanu-El to Bella Baer, a member of the Class of 1882.

dispense with the wearing of a *talis* at Emanu-El. He also held the first Emanu-El Confirmation service for a class of three girls and two boys.

Rabbi Spitz ultimately encountered stormy times. The Board wanted him to leave, but the membership supported him, overcoming the Board's decision, thereby causing the resignation of its prestigious founder and first president,

Rabbi Moritz Spitz

Rabbi I.S. Moses

David Adler. The rift came as a huge blow to the congregation, precipitating the announcement by Rabbi Spitz that he was leaving for a pulpit in St. Louis. Adler, of course, eventually returned to membership and was reelected to the presidency an additional three times.

Times were no less turbulent with the 1879 arrival of Rabbi I.S. Moses, who unleashed a torrent of criticism by performing an intermarriage in Wauwatosa to avoid a congregational rule that all marriages should be performed within the city limits. Again congregants came to the defense of their rabbi, lauding him for his spirit of independence. Later, he again incurred the wrath of the Board when he slapped the 13-year old son of one of the trustees. A conciliatory address calmed the situation and Rabbi Moses continued to serve through 1887.

Rabbi Sigmund Hecht then arrived at Emanu-El after 12 years' service in Montgomery, Alabama, where he simultaneously earned a Doctor of Divinity degree from the University of Alabama. A believer in non-congregational work in both the Jewish and secular communities in addition to his rabbinic duties, he attained prominence and popularity here for his work with Associated Charities of Wisconsin, the Wisconsin Humane Society, and for his service as president of Jewish Relief. He also served on the Board of Governors of the Hebrew Union College and as treasurer of the Central Conference of American Rabbis. He also published a textbook that was widely adopted for use in many Sabbath Schools of the time.

Three events marked his decade of service at Emanu-El. In 1892, the Great Fair of Temple Emanu-El was organized by the Ladies Society, raising $12,000 for the erection of Emanu-El Hall, the multi-purpose addition to house the Sabbath School, the Jewish Mission School for teaching the

Large families were common in the late 19th century and helped to increase the local Jewish population. Leopold H. Harris, B'ne Jeshurun president in 1891-92 (fourth from right with beard),with his wife, Esther, had seven children. Great-Granddaughter, Audrey Keyes remains an Emanu-El B'ne Jeshurun member and also served on the Board of Trustees.

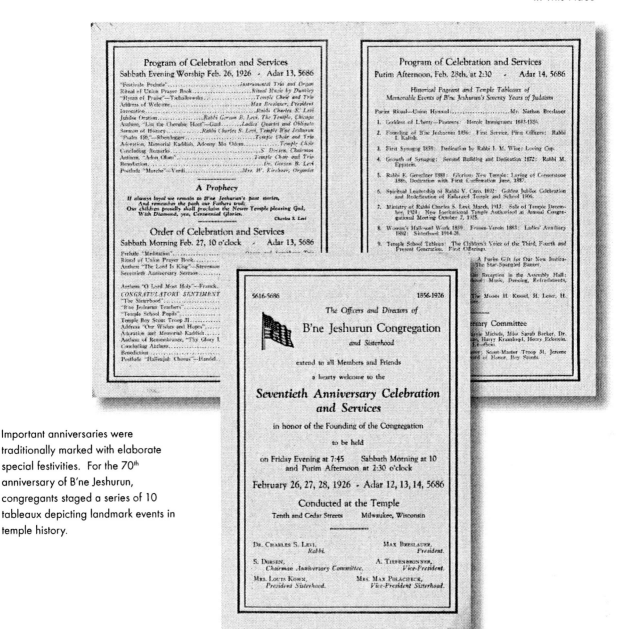

Important anniversaries were traditionally marked with elaborate special festivities. For the 70th anniversary of B'ne Jeshurun, congregants staged a series of 10 tableaux depicting landmark events in temple history.

children of the poor and Russian Night School for teaching English to the increasing multitude of Russian immigrants.

Now in its 25th year in 1894, the congregation planned a Silver Anniversary Commemoration. Rabbi Hecht headed an afternoon of prayer, music and speeches including a sermon by Isaac Mayer Wise and an address by the redoubtable David Adler, who had been active in Emanu-El affairs for the entire quarter century of its existence and who was yet again congregational president.

It was five years hence on October 27,1899 when Rabbi Hecht preached his last Friday night sermon after asking to be released from his contract. Before leaving, he compiled a "little history" of his highly productive decade in Milwaukee. In it he recounted with great candor the highlights and disappointments of his active years here.

He applauded the membership of 90-120 families that he described as "small, but far-reaching in influence." It was a mantel Emanu-El would continue to wear throughout

Rabbi Sigmund Hecht

most of the upcoming century. He was proud that they were among the first U.S. congregations to use the new Union Prayer Book. He praised the efforts of the volunteer teachers in the Sabbath School. Unlike his predecessor, Rabbi Moses, he stood strongly against mixed marriages. Although he discouraged conversion, he actually converted four individuals. He believed that children should begin Sabbath School at an early age, but he opposed Bar Mitzvah. He did not think a boy of 13 was spiritually

It was the practice in both congregations for members to purchase a specific pew in the synagogue. Often the most desirable locations brought higher prices. This very formal document filed in 1902 granted Charles and Carrie Polacheck ownership of Pew #64 at B'ne Jeshurun for $25.

mature, and he felt children needed to continue their Jewish education after age 13. He thus succeeded in convincing many parents that Confirmation was more effective than Bar Mitzvah. He confirmed a total of 52 young people— girls as well as boys—during his stay here. Bar Mitzvah thus eliminated, it remained outside the program for over half a century until its reintroduction in 1951.

Rabbi Hecht's "little history" book criticized parents who were not sending their children to Religious School and expressed the view that the congregation should more aggressively encourage unmarried men to participate in synagogue affairs. He chided his congregants about poor attendance at services, which he described as having often "included only the rabbi, the choir, the president, vice-president and some of our good ladies."

Rabbi Hecht opposed intermarriage because "it would mean the gradual weakening and destruction of the religion." He was an early opponent of Zionism. He became dissatisfied with the attitudes of the congregation, blaming them for "sacrilege and blasphemy, callous indifference and apathy."

From 1869 until the onset of the 20th century, Emanu-El on the East Side and B'ne Jeshurun on the West Side both experienced steady growth, each managing building campaigns that culminated in new synagogue structures. B'ne Jeshurun's facility was erected in 1886 at 10th and Cedar Sts., now the site of the Milwaukee County Courthouse, while Emanu-El had occupied its new building at Martin and State Sts. since 1872.

As intended by its organizers, Emanu-El was less traditional in its practices than its West Side counterpart. A later observer, characterizing the two groups during the last 30 years of the 19th century, described B'ne Jeshurun as "financially comfortable," while Emanu-El was "opulent." Both customarily sold pews for the use of wealthy congregants, a common practice at the time. Pews were priced according to location and prime seats carried considerable prestige for the buyers.

B'ne Jeshurun Confirmation Class of 1905. With Rabbi Caro are: (Standing l to r) Julius Goodman, Ben Matras, Sam Spero, Milton Spitz, Robert Kohn, Walter Mahler. (Seated l to r) Mamie Fredman Blink, Adline Seyliner, Esther Leavet, Rabbi Caro, Rose Birnbaum, Florence Rosenberg, and Addie Mandel Kohn.

On the 50th anniversary of B'ne Jeshurun, the temple was rededicated in 1906 with an elaborate program under the direction of Rabbi Caro.

Worship in the two congregations remained similar although B'ne Jeshurun retained a slightly more traditional brand of Judaism than Emanu-El, where services were conducted entirely in English and approved the custom of worshipping with uncovered heads. Although from its inception, Emanu-El had made English its preferred language, it did not become the language of record at B'ne Jeshurun until 1905.

Soon after its founding, Emanu-El became a very active group. Occupying its new home for just three years, they hosted conventions of the prestigious Union of American Hebrew Congregations and the Central Conference of American Rabbis.

Emanu-El in the 20th Century

The 20th century began at Emanu-El with the arrival of 26-year old Rabbi Julius Meyer, the first Hebrew Union College graduate to occupy this pulpit. Like Rabbi Hecht, Rabbi Meyer found his members indifferent to their religion. Discouraged, he left the active rabbinate in 1904 to enter the business field. His successor, Rabbi Samuel

Rabbi Julius Meyer

Rabbi Samuel Hirshberg

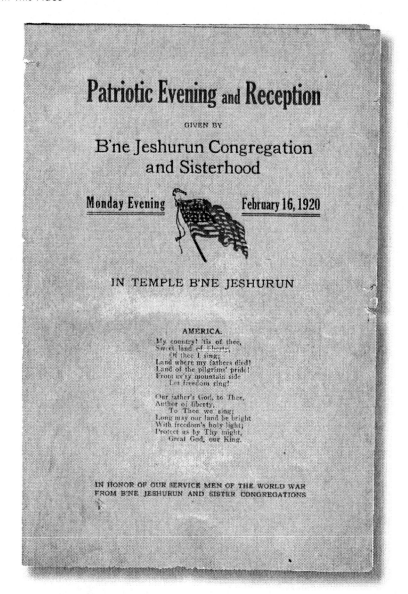

Patriotism was a constant theme throughout the nineteenth and early twentieth centuries. This special service arranged at B'ne Jeshurun by Rabbi Levi was held just three months after the end of World War I.

Hirshberg, accepted the challenge and opened a new era that would last for nearly half a century. He attended Harvard and was ordained at the Hebrew Union College. Molding a classical Reform congregation, he was a non-Zionist who believed strongly that Jews should aid in the social and economic problems of the day. Rabbi Hirshberg remained at Emanu-El over a 43-year tenure and continued to serve as Rabbi Emeritus until his death.

Temples frequently wind up with unusual problems. This Prohibition period application signed in 1920 by Rabbi Hirshberg requests permission to purchase "one gallon of grape wine for sacramental or like religious rites".

In his inaugural sermon, Rabbi Hirshberg said he had been warned "how difficult a minister's task here must be." He had learned "that his temple possesses...a great many people...who take delight in boasting that they are as little Jewish as possible."

Under his leadership, Emanu-El flourished and celebrated its 50-year anniversary in 1919 with a banquet at the Pfister Hotel's elegant Fern Room. Toastmaster for the evening was president A.L. Saltzstein. Daniel P. Hayes, an

Executive Board member of the Union of American Hebrew Congregations, was the main speaker. Rabbi Charles Levi, rabbi of the mother congregation, B'ne Jeshurun, gave the invocation.

In the same year, negotiations were concluded for a new building on Kenwood Blvd. Land had first been purchased on Hackett Ave., but that parcel was soon considered inappropriate by the Building Committee due to noise and traffic conditions from a very active neighboring church. Reconsidering this location proved to be fortunate insight, since the age of the automobile was at hand, increasing an existing parking problem that would have quickly doomed the site. The Hackett land was sold and a larger, nearby Kenwood site was purchased from the Cummings family.

Emanu-El laid the cornerstone for a new Kenwood Blvd. temple at ceremonies in 1923. The building now houses Fine Arts functions of University of Wisconsin-Milwaukee, but still opens its doors to the congregation for High Holiday services.

Controversy has obtained even since original organization in 1856. This resolution passed unanimously by the B'ne Jeshurun Sisterhood in 1926 urges the Board to reconsider acceptance of Rabbi Levi's resignation in favor of a full congregational vote.

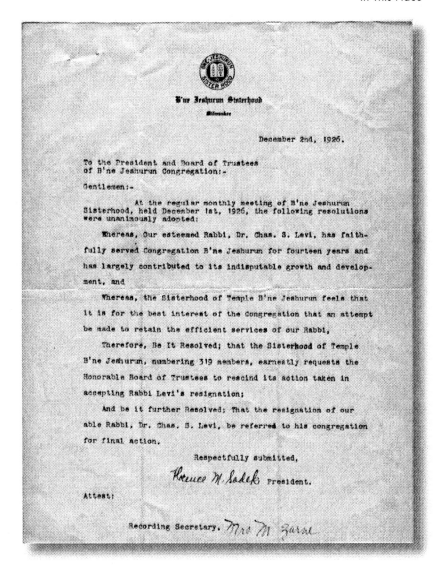

Construction began on the building that would house the congregation for the remainder of the century. Memorial Day, May 30, 1922, was the day the cornerstone was laid for the landmark Kenwood building that would stand across from the present University of Wisconsin-Milwaukee.

Rabbi Hirshberg, who had been warned by colleagues about accepting Emanu-El's pulpit, now received congratulations from throughout the world of Reform

31

TO THE BOARD OF DIRECTORS OF

Congregation B'ne Jeshurun

Milwaukee, Wisconsin, *Sept.* 192*6.*

I hereby make application for a Class **Young Men's** *Membership in Congregation B'ne Jeshurun.*

*If my application is accepted by the Board of Directors I agree to pay membership dues from the date hereof to September 1st, 192*7*, and annually thereafter at the rate of $* 24 *per annum. I agree to pay my dues six months in advance and to abide by all rules, laws and regulations of the Congregation.*

Signed **Nathan P. Breslauer**

Recommended by **Rabbi Charles S. Levi** *Address* **768 Maryland Ave**

Applications for membership were formal but simple. Nathan Breslauer applied for a Young Men's membership in 1927 at an annual dues of $24.

Judaism. From Rabbi Barnett Brickner came this message: "When a new temple is built, it is like lighting a new torch kindled by the fire of the old altar to spread the light of the ideals of Judaism and to comfort by the warmth which that light generates."

Rabbi Emeritus Henry Berkowitz of Rodeph Shalom, Philadelphia, sent this letter: "There is something of special significance in this event which resounds to the honor of all American Israel, an achievement that needs special recognition. Back in 1889, Milwaukee was considered a very difficult Jewish community that displayed a skeptical attitude toward religion. The earnestness and zeal that you have successfully fostered evokes my sincere and cordial admiration."

Report cards—ever the dread of Religious School students—have aways been employed as a benchmark of progress for both parents and students. These are examples of the style used at B'ne Jeshurun in 1926.

In exactly one year—May 30,1923—the Kenwood building was dedicated. It was an impressive columned structure with a high dome frescoed with symbols of the Jewish holidays. Again, Reform Judaism across America took note. Rabbi Hirshberg attracted many congratulatory letters including one from Nathan Krass, rabbi of New York's Temple Emanu-El. Another from Rabbi Joseph Henry Stolz said: "If an entirely different spirit towards Judaism has during the past two decades appeared in Milwaukee, and if it is no longer said that when God wants to punish a rabbi, he sends him to Milwaukee, I know you have been responsible more than anyone else in doing this."

During the 1920's, a few changes and innovations began to emerge. A bit of Hebrew was introduced into the liturgy. Sisterhood Sabbath began as early as 1923 and a new organ for the new building was dedicated that same year. High Holy Day cards of admission began circa 1924. Families who had customarily purchased pews gave up their seats. An open seating policy existed for most services, but a

Rabbi Joseph L. Baron

system of assigned seating was instituted for the High Holy
Days.

With 400 member families in 1926, Emanu-El was large
enough to engage young Rabbi Joseph L. Baron as assistant
to Rabbi Hirshberg. Rabbi Baron came to Milwaukee after
six years in a Davenport, Iowa pulpit. A descendant of the
Vilna Gaon, the famous 18th century genius of Torah study,
Rabbi Baron studied at a New York yeshiva and the Jewish
Theological Seminary while simultaneously earning a
degree at Columbia University. He was also ordained at the
Hebrew Union College in 1920 and was very accomplished
in Hebrew and several European languages.

Meanwhile, B'ne Jeshurun in the 1920's began to feel cramped in its regal 1886 building on 10th and Cedar. There was, however, considerable disagreement on a new location. Should it be on the East Side or the West Side? A traditional theme had returned. A small group even lobbied for a South Side location. The matter came to a head in 1927 when the synagogue received word from Milwaukee County that the existing building would have to be razed to make room for the County Courthouse.

With Emanu-El in its fifth year of residence in the spacious Kenwood Blvd. location, there were those who

Bottom Left: Official notification to the State of Wisconsin and Milwaukee County of the merger agreement between Emanu-El and B'ne Jeshurun in 1927.

Bottom Right: Original edited text of a letter from Emanu-El announcing the return of Hebrew instruction in the Religious School. A return post card permitted parents to reject the instruction if they so desired.

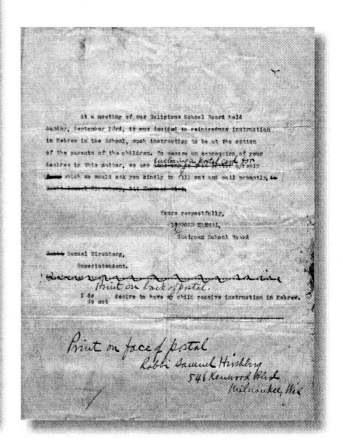

believed consolidation was a more practical solution than construction of an entire new B'ne Jeshurun, despite the fact that approval for fund-raising had already been given.

Extensive discussions between the two groups resulted in a lengthy meeting on September 15, 1927. The two congregations decided to consolidate and to be known as Congregation Emanu-El B'ne Jeshurun. At the same meeting, new by-laws were approved and Rabbi Hirshberg was elected Senior Rabbi. Rabbi Baron was elected assistant. The plea issued by Rabbi Isaac Mayer Wise 78 years earlier would now become a reality. Milwaukee's Reform Jewish community would be united in a single congregation.

Bolstered in size by the consolidation, the merged congregation continued to grow and in 1929 Rabbi Hirshberg was feted for 25 years of service at a congregational dinner in temple's social hall. A.L. Saltzstein was again president and acted as toastmaster. Speeches were given by Samuel Hirshberg's father and brother, rabbis respectively in New Brunswick, N.J. and at Chicago's highly respected Temple Shalom. Rabbi Samuel Hirshberg was again

Temple Split Over Merger

Sentinel 3/15/27

Many B'ne Jeshurun Members Would Join Emanu-El *Journal*

Members of the congregation of Temple B'ne Jeshurun, Tenth and Cedar sts., one of Milwaukee's oldest and largest Jewish groups, are divided over a proposal, backed by part of the members, that the congregation give up plans for a new temple and merge forces with their more liberal brethren at Temple Emanu-El.

A lively contest is forecast for Thursday night when members of the west side congregation are to meet to vote on the proposed merger. If decided upon, this will mean that plans for a new B'ne Jeshurun temple, now under way, will be dropped. The present temple property has been sold to the city as a part of the new civic center site.

Sigmund Dorsen, treasurer of the congregation, declared Monday that rumors of the merger were "the result of gossip." He said that members of B'ne Jeshurun congregation are still planning to build a $300,000 temple, and said that the meeting Thursday night has been called to consider further details of the building plans. The selection of a site for the new building will be one of the propositions put before the members at that time, Mr. Dorsen said.

Members Are Divided

According to a high official in the B'ne Jeshurun congregation the opposition to the proposed merger comes, for the most part, from members of the congregation, about 145 in number, who live on the west and south sides and who wish to build a new temple somewhere near the present site. There are 110 members of the temple, he said, who live on the east side and lean toward the merger which, they feel, will make the erection of a new temple unnecessary.

Rabbi Samuel Hirshberg of Temple Emanu-El said Monday that the merger was being considered and had been discussed at a joint committee meeting attended by representatives of both congregations. Members of the joint committee, he said, now will present the proposal to the members of each temple, asking a vote on the plan.

Have Temple Fund

Mr. Dorsen admitted that the merger had been considered in a committee conference but said the conference had been "unofficial."

At the annual meeting of the B'ne Jeshurun congregation at the Hotel Astor several months ago, members of the congregation pledged several thousand dollars to supplement a nucleus for their new building fund, obtained from the sale of the Cedar st. site.

VOTE MERGER OF JEWISH TEMPLES

Wisconsin News Mar 25/1927

The congregation of Temple B'ne Jeshurun voted overwhelmingly last night in favor of the proposed merger with Temple Emanu-El congregation, largest liberal Jewish group in the state.

The vote of the congregation, which is the oldest among the Jewish organizations in the Northwest, was 154 to 22 in favor of consolidation. It was necessary to throw out two ballots, and seventy-two proxies were voted.

Arthur Polacheck, president; Sig Dorsen, treasurer, and Henry V. Meissner, director and attorney, were appointed as a committee to meet with a similar committee to be chosen by the Temple Emanu-El congregation when that membership follows the expected court of approving the proposal to amalgamate. The joint committee will carry out the legal details necessary to the perfection of the consolidation.

The combined congregations will number about eight hundred, of which five hundred already are members of Emanu-El, which is an offspring of Temple B'ne Jeshurun by a liberalist faction.

Considerable publicity surrounded the controversy over merger of the two Reform congregations. Articles from the Milwaukee Journal detail both controversy and resolution.

honored at the Golden Anniversary of his ordination in 1941.

On his retirement in 1947, Rabbi Hirshberg turned over to Rabbi Baron a more dedicated membership than the widely criticized group he inherited on his arrival 43 years earlier. Rabbi Baron was immediately able to quicken the pace of congregational life. He founded a Men's Club (now Brotherhood), sharpened administrative procedures, improved the library, and instituted a museum of Jewish artifacts (the Joseph L. Baron Museum now bears his name). There was an education program for adults, a Junior Congregation for post-Confirmation teenagers and a Cradle Roll for the even younger set. Annual Sabbath services celebrating Consecration of new Religious School students and Homecoming for college students were added. So long was the list of activities that the temple bulletin had to be increased to weekly issues.

In his early years here, Rabbi Baron earned a Ph.D degree from the

University of Chicago, taught at the neighboring Milwaukee State Teachers College (now University of Wisconsin-Milwaukee) and lectured at the Milwaukee County Council of Churches Leadership School. He found time to author three books, "A Treasury of Jewish Quotations", "Candles in the Night" and "Stars and Sand" in addition to articles in encyclopedias, scientific journals and popular magazines. He served on the Union of American Hebrew Congregations Board of Governors and the Central Conference of American Rabbis. Locally, he provided the impetus for the founding of the Wisconsin Council for Jewish Learning.

Faced with the impending retirement of Rabbi Hirshberg in 1947, the congregation hired Rabbi Harry B. Pastor in 1947 to serve as assistant to Rabbi Baron. In

With merger, the size of Confirmation classes grew considerably as evidenced by this first combined class of 1928.

Front Row (l-r): David Gelder, Mildred Rosenthal, Geraldine Smith, Ruth Berkwich, Evelyn Brin, Bertha Louise Seelig, Sylvia Kripke, Sarah Schwartzenfeld, Elizabeth Neu, Bertram Rubenstein. Second Row: Armin Kaufer, Irene Broude, Jane Goldstein, Ruth Greenwald, Margaret Kupper, Cyrene Kirsch, Harriet Kesselman, Evelyn Kaiser, Ruth Albert, Carolyn Feinstein, Robert Hammerschlag. Third Row: Rabbi Hirshberg, Dorothy Saltzstein, Clifford Bitker, Milton Ehrlich, Myron Waybick, Roy Shapiro, Marvin Glasspiegel, Alfred Wahlberg, Bernard Hankin, Rabbi Baron. Fourth Row: Harold Albert, James Merske, Howard Weiner, Robert Apple, Oscar Brachman, Jr., Samuel Langer, Robert Pentler, Nathan Schlossman.
Not picutred: Milton Feinberg, Ruth Goldman, Stanley Meyer, Harold Ruwin, Charlotte Teweles

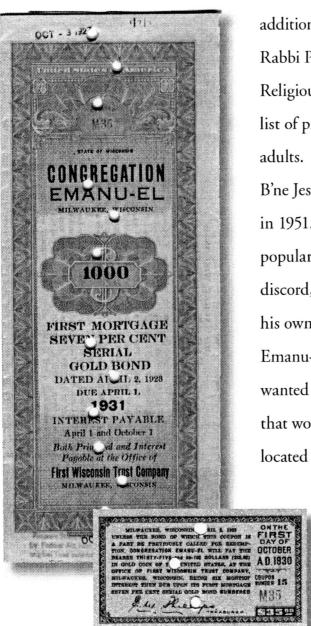

Financing for Emanu-El's move to Kenwood Blvd. included a bond issue to which members could subscribe and receive semi-annual interest payments in exchange for the loan. This cancelled bond was redeemed after just three years and may have been donated back to the congregation as a pledge fulfillment.

addition to his liturgical work, Rabbi Pastor was responsible for the Religious School and the increasing list of programs involving young adults. He remained at Emanu-El B'ne Jeshurun for four years, leaving in 1951. Despite considerable popularity, he left in a measure of discord, ready to serve as rabbi of his own congregation. A group of Emanu-El B'ne Jeshurun members wanted a Reform congregation that would be more conveniently located in the suburbs, which were attracting a rapidly increasing Jewish population. They founded Congregation Shalom and retained Rabbi Pastor, who would remain in the community for the rest of his life. The same year increasing health problems caused Rabbi Baron to retire to emeritus status.

The World War II years
had brought both demographic
and emotional changes to the
Milwaukee community. A
new generation of Reform
Jews arose as many West Side
families moved to the East Side.
Sensitized by the war and the
Holocaust, they were turning
a bit more to the symbols of
traditional Judaism. Hebrew
was more commonly heard,
both in spoken prayer and in
music. Although a 1930 report
in the Milwaukee Sentinel quoted

Mrs. A.W. (Rose) Rich founded the Ladies Relief Sewing Society in 1869. Mrs. Rich believed "women of leisure time ought to give up a little of their time to alleviate the suffering of the poor and needy." Although the society became a member of Federated Jewish Charities in 1902, it served as the predecessor of the Sisterhood organizations that flourished at both Emanu-El and B'ne Jeshurun.

president A. L. Saltzstein as lamenting the loss of "emotional
appeal through over rationalization" and calling for "a
return to some of the pomp and ceremony of Orthodoxy,"
his proposal for adding a cantor went unrealized until the
first cantor of the 20th century, Anthony Scott, was added
to the staff in 1948 and the education of both adults and
children was intensified.

Meanwhile, the congregation faced the problem of
finding a Senior Rabbi for the first time since 1904. The
complexity of programming that had grown over the years
required a broad national search. As a result, Herbert

The popular Junior Congregation program fulfilled the long hope of the rabbis for continuation of education past Confirmation age. Combining social activities with instruction, the series resulted in these 34 students reaching the "high school graduation" level in 1954.

Friedman of Temple Emanu-El in Denver, was called to the Milwaukee pulpit. His tenure in Denver had been interrupted by a tour as a chaplain with the Army of Occupation in Germany and for a time he was the only Jewish chaplain in Berlin.

In 1946, Chaplain Friedman was asked by Rabbi Phillip Bernstein, advisor for Jewish affairs to the commanding general, to serve as his aide on a trip to Poland, resulting in a subsequent reassignment to Frankfurt as the permanent assistant to Rabbi Bernstein. Until his return to the United States the following year, he served in that same capacity, working primarily with displaced persons.

41

Later he was asked to accompany Henry Morganthau, then chairman of the United Jewish Appeal, to speak about the situation of Jewish displaced persons in Germany and Austria.

At the invitation of Israeli Prime Minister Ben Gurion, he attended the Jerusalem conference that launched the 1950 Israel Bond drive just two years into Israel's existence. As chairman of the Central Conference of American Rabbis' Committee for Projects on Israel, he led a group of American Reform rabbis to Israel for a five-week study institute.

When Rabbi Friedman arrived to lead Emanu-El B'ne Jeshurun, he quickly became known for his fiery and passionate preaching style. Temple attendance mushroomed

Rabbi Herbert Friedman

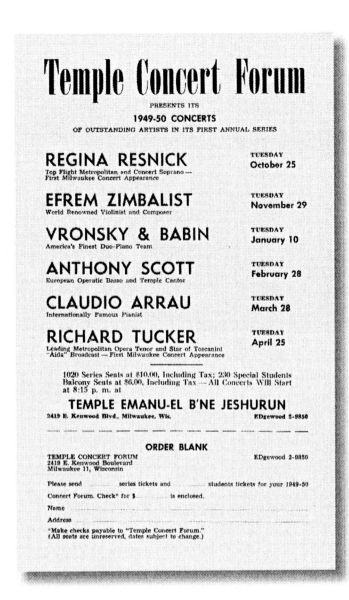

A 1949-50 concert series was typical of the secular cultural activities thought to be attractive programming. These six concerts brought to our sanctuary six exceptionally talented and well-know artists. Series seats were just $10.

with everyone eager to hear his sermons. At his installation service people were asked to bring their own prayer books in anticipation of an overflow crowd. An installation banquet was later held at the Schroeder Hotel.

Measured by modern local standards, his 4-year tenure was short, but packed with changes reflective of the continued post war attitudes. Throughout the country, younger Reform rabbis were reintroducing increasingly traditional practices to their services and educational programs. Strengthened by the emergence of a new and vital Israel, Hebrew education of both children and adults received new emphasis. A Bar Mitzvah program was reinstituted after absence of nearly an entire generation. The first Bar Mitzvah was Michael Benjamin Laiken, whose father George Laiken prepared him for the event held June 2, 1952.

It marked a clear step into a new post-war era when 13-year old Dinah Berland became the first Bat Mitzvah in the history of the congregation two years later. Berland is now a widely published poet and working as an editor for Getty Publications, Los Angeles. In a memoir, she recalled, "I had the distinction of being the first girl trained at my temple to become a Bat Mitzvah. When that day arrived I stood on the *bimah* in my pink pique dress and white patent leather shoes, stepped on a footstool and had the honor of reading from the Torah before a congregation of family and friends. After completing my reading and delivering my speech I found myself standing in front of the rabbi, my eyes at the level of his tie clip. As Rabbi Friedman, a tall handsome man with a sonorous voice, placed his hands lightly above my head to bestow the priestly blessing, I felt something I had never felt before and had no words for. It was a sensation of pure absolute love. I was deeply moved."

The State of Israel is Born

When in 1948, the United Nations proclaimed the establishment of the new State of Israel, the action immediately had a profound impact on American Judaism. Very quickly it rendered moot the long-smoldering Zionist vs. Anti-Zionist issue, thereby creating unity from a long-simmering debate in Jewish communities nationwide.

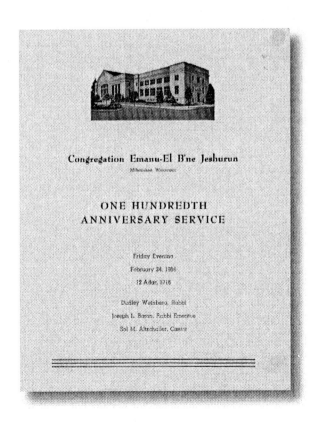

Dudley Weinberg

Dedication to survival of the new state became the common
goal and fundraising for the benefit of our new homeland
became the sharp focus, overshadowing congregational
concerns.

Rabbi Friedman, a worker dedicated to displaced persons
following the war, yearned to return to aid those who
had found their way to Israel and who would become the
cornerstone of an new immigrant pioneer society there. In
1955, he accepted appointment as executive vice-chairman of
the national United Jewish Appeal. Later, in 1970 he became
its executive chairman and moved with his family to Israel.

Again a search committee was formed. Their selection
was Dudley Weinberg, a forceful Jewish spokesman and
community leader in his nine years at Temple Ohabei

Shalom in Boston. Informed that Rabbi Weinberg would be his successor, Rabbi Friedman said he "has my wholehearted approval. He is the finest man we could get, and he has a magnificent reputation among his colleagues. He will represent the congregation well and push it to even greater heights."

Rabbi Weinberg graduated Phi Beta Kappa from Carleton College where he also taught in the German department. He was ordained at the Hebrew Union College in Cincinnati, taking class honors for his academic record as well as his preaching.

He served Temple Israel in Memphis until he volunteered to serve as an Army chaplain in 1943. He served in the Pacific theater in New Guinea and in the Philippines, where in addition to his front-line service he organized a large Passover seder and helped to raise money to rebuild a Manila synagogue that had been demolished by the Japanese. He completed his service with the rank of Major and was awarded a Bronze Star, which is conferred for "distinguished or meritorious service during combat," having been twice commended by his commanding general for his front line ministry. He was later chosen to give the dedicatory prayer for the carillon at the National Cathedral in Washington, D.C. Among those in attendance was President Harry S. Truman.

Arriving in Milwaukee in 1955, Rabbi Weinberg quickly established his forcefulness as a visionary community leader. Deeply interested in the broad scope of local religious and cultural life, he was an ardent supporter of art and music, bringing to the synagogue dance performances and orchestral appearances, sometimes integrating them into Sabbath or other religious services. The programs were expressions of his philosophy that the building was as much a house of community as it was a house of worship.

Negro Problem Can Set Off Explosion, Says Rabbi Weinberg

"He is the refuge of the oppressed, the deliverer of the persecuted."

Members of Congregation Emanu-El B'ne Jeshurun recited that passage from their prayer books Friday night as they heard how the tragic story of the Negro problem in the United States "could set off an explosion."

The Negro issue is a tragic one, particularly at this time of world tension, the congregation was told by Rabbi Dudley Weinberg.

LAUDS COURT RULING

"If the Supreme Court had acted otherwise, however; our standing among nations would have shriveled before our eyes," the rabbi said, adding:

"But we can be proud because it was a pronouncement to the world that America is taking one more great stride forward toward perfect democracy."

He praised the "courageous, unyielding stand" taken by many Negroes and some whites in the deep South.

CITED COURAGE

Speaking from the altar during the solemn Sabbath services, Rabbi Weinberg cited the courage of the Catholic bishop of Raleigh, N. C., and a Jewish rabbi in New Orleans, who have been outspoken in their fight for the rights of Negroes.

But, he warned, the problem is one for everyone in the country, not just the South. It is easy for us to speak from afar, but we must recognize that wisdom and patience alone will bring about equality which all men must share.

'SOUTH AFRAID'

He said white people in the South fight equality because they are afraid. "The sins they fear will be committed by Negroes are the sins they themselves have committed against the Negroes in the past," he said.

"I believe the barriers can be removed and inequality eliminated, but it must be accomplished through intelligence and understanding," he said. "The people must be taught that no one has anything to fear from equality under the law."

Milw Sentinel   March 24-1955

Sensitized to race relations problems while still in Boston, Rabbi Weinberg brought his concerns with him and immediately went to work to promote racial equality here. This article appeared soon after the Supreme Court banned school segregation.

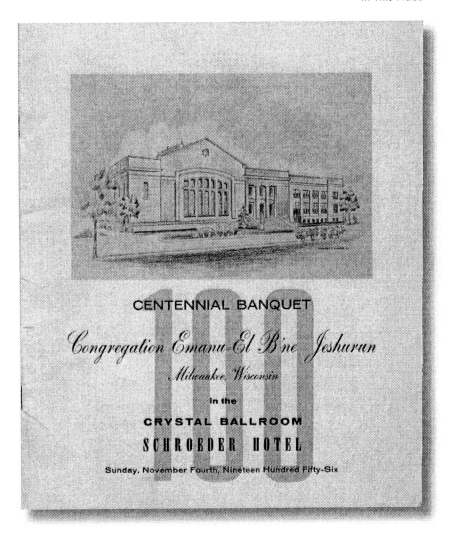

His years were those of considerable racial strife in the city and he believed the Jewish community owed a great measure of support for civil rights. Frequently outspoken, his support resonated clearly among congregants as well as in the general community. He was a prime mover of the Greater Milwaukee Conference on Religion and Race, serving first as its founder and later as president.

"The Negro issue is a tragic one particularly at this time of world tension," Rabbi Weinberg expounded in a sermon shortly after his 1955 arrival, which was very early in America's tussle with segregation issues. It was just one year after the Supreme Court ruled school segregation unconstitutional. He warned the problem was national in scope and not regionally limited to the South. "It is easy for us to speak from afar, but we must recognize that wisdom and patience alone will bring about equality which all men must share". It was his early salvo in a battle that would continue throughout his life. As the campaign for racial equality heated up in future years, he supported Father James Groppi in a staunch, high-profile battle for a city law guaranteeing open housing.

In 1964 he invited Archbishop William A. Cousins to the Emanu-El B'ne Jeshurun pulpit to speak about the historic interfaith reforms established for the Catholic Church by Vatican II. It was the first time that a ranking Catholic prelate ever appeared in a local synagogue.

The following year, a congregational dinner honored his 10 years of service here, the 25th anniversary of his marriage

Another First !

BY
THE MEN'S CLUB
OF CONGREGATION
EMANU-EL B'NE JESHURUN

YOU ARE CORDIALLY INVITED TO PARTAKE IN

"A WEEK-END
with
—— RABBI DUDLEY WEINBERG" ——

A 48 hour period of contemplative study, discussion, worship and conviviality is being planned by your Men's Club.

WHEN: LATE FRIDAY AFTERNOON SEPTEMBER 28, 1956
THROUGH SUNDAY AFTERNOON SEPTEMBER 30, 1956

WHERE: SIEBKENS RESORT, ELKHART LAKE, WISCONSIN

HOW MUCH: $35.00 INCLUDES 6 SUMPTUOUS MEALS, GRATUITIES, HEATED TWIN BEDDED OR PRIVATE ROOMS, AND SEPARATE BATHS.

WHY: TO AFFORD US THE OPPORTUNITY OF GETTING BETTER ACQUAINTED WITH EACH OTHER, WITH OUR RABBI, OUR CANTOR, AND WITH OUR FAITH.

YOU are being given this thrilling opportunity on a "first come first served" basis. We positively cannot allow guest privileges -- nor can we accommodate more than 30 men! (no wives.)

Please send your check to the undersigned at once and indicate if you wish to share a room and with whom. Also, whether you are driving and are willing to take others with you.

Marvin L. Kohner
4847 No. Marlborough Dr.

Soon after arriving in Milwaukee, Rabbi Weinberg invited the Men's Club (now Brotherhood) to a "Weekend with Rabbi Weinberg". A popular event, perhaps because two nights and six meals at an Elkhart Lake Resort was priced at only $35.

to his wife, Marian, and the 25th anniversary of his
ordination, for which he was awarded a Doctor of Divinity
degree from the Hebrew Union College.

An ardent Zionist, Rabbi Weinberg was a firm believer
in the importance of elevating standards of Jewish
education. In 1974, he emphasized the need for a Jewish
day school under liberal auspices. A day school was
needed, according to Weinberg, because "the community
has molded into an America where Jews are losing their
heritage." A liberal day school would offer children an
education and commitment to their faith and heritage as
well as high-level secular instruction.

The visit of Milwaukee's Archbishop William Cousins to the congregation was a momentous occasion. It was considered the first ever visit of a high member of the Catholic clergy to a synagogue here.

Among his favorite activities was a frequent presence in the interfaith community. He joined the faculty of Marquette University and became the first rabbi to teach a course in Jewish studies there. The course was sponsored by the Jewish Chautauqua Society, interfaith arm of the National Federation of Brotherhoods and participation in the course was continued by Rabbi Weinberg's successors. He also helped to educate Milwaukee's Christian clergy, often speaking to clerical groups and by hosting an annual Institute on Judaism for local pastors.

As had been the case with his recent predecessors, Rabbi Weinberg was appointed to the rabbinic Board of Alumni Overseers of the Hebrew Union College (by then

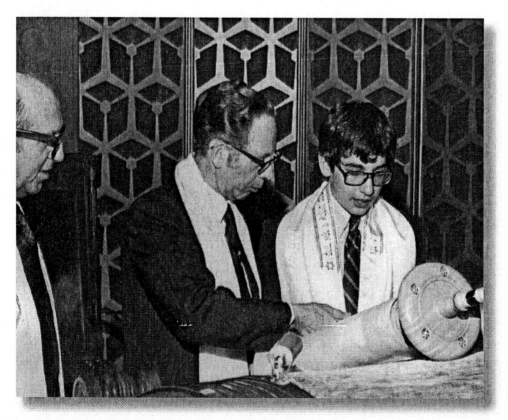

Hebrew instruction, reinstitued in the 1940's, has become a vital part of the Religious School program. Bar Mitzvah ceremonies such as that conducted by Rabbi Weinberg of Richard Fromstein in 1973 are extremely common.

merged with New York's Jewish Institute of Religion) and
the Board of Trustees of the Union of American Hebrew
Congregations.

Wars in Israel in 1956, 1967 and 1973 had consumed
the entire focus of worldwide Jewry and the needs of
congregations moved to the back burner. By the mid-
1970's, however, long delayed local community needs took
on a more urgent priority. Almost a half-century had passed
since the Kenwood building, once considered spacious was
first occupied. Increased membership resulting from the
consolidation of two congregations, aggressively expanded
educational activities and broadened general programming
had long since rendered the venerable structure inadequate
and the Board of Trustees faced the critical, frequently
recurring question: Expand at the Kenwood location or
move to the suburbs, where Congregation Shalom and
Congregation Sinai were already present?

Sensing the movement of Jewish families to the suburbs
as early as 1956, an earlier board had purchased a tract
of land in Fox Point in the event future relocation would
become appropriate. Congregation Sinai, however, had later
located on property immediately adjacent to that land and
trustees were reluctant to place two Reform congregations
virtually as "next door neighbors". The option to Kenwood
expansion became selling the land and searching for a
different, suitable location.

In modern times, Religious School instruction has become increasingly professional and effective as evidenced by the intensity of this young student. Hebrew instruction, long ignored by Reform Judaism, has been an important part of the instruction since the 1940's.

There was considerable support for expansion. The Kenwood building was a neighbor to rapidly growing University of Wisconsin-Milwaukee, which offered an academic ambience with extensive library and research facilities. Among the members was a valued group of university teachers, professors and administrators. Removal to the suburbs would leave the city unrepresented by Reform Judaism. Because the congregation was the oldest and largest in the area, it wore the mantle of leadership in the eyes of the city establishment. The board felt a measure of obligation to continue fulfilling that role.

Still, the Kenwood site was inconvenient to the majority of members. Those with children in the after-school Hebrew program were reluctant to send them via school bus in the cold of winter to an additional study session that would continue to occupy them well after dark. Families found it difficult to observe a Sabbath dinner at home and return to the city for Friday night services.

The Board of Trustees ultimately recommended, and a congregational vote accepted, a decision to expand the existing facility, adding space for youth activities, library, and badly needed classrooms and office space at a cost of $1,000,000. The land acquired in 1956 at a cost of $50,000 was sold to private developers for $500,000. A fundraising drive produced commitments for the full expansion cost and the proceeds from the land sale were, at the suggestion of Rabbi Weinberg, placed in a trust administered by a specially appointed group of trustees for the purpose of financing program development. While the trust financed development of numerous unusual and challenging program ideas, the critical financial needs of future years ultimately resulted in the commingling of the trust money with general funds.

Financing and contracting arrangements for the expansion having been completed by August, 1974, Rabbi Weinberg and president Ben Chernov turned the first shovels of dirt at a groundbreaking ceremony. Designating the project a milestone, Chernov said it represented a commitment to retain Reform Judaism in the city. When Mayor Henry Maier spoke, he praised the decision to remain in the city rather than relocating to Fox Point.

"This is a vote of confidence," he said "and a symbol of the permanence of our city."

The expansion completed in 1975, health problems kept Rabbi Weinberg away from his pulpit for most of the following year and he passed away in 1976. He was eulogized by Rabbi Arthur Lelyveld, president of the Central Conference of American Rabbis, and by Rabbi Louis Silverman, his longtime friend and colleague. His associate, Rabbi Francis Barry Silberg, described him a " the Jewish soul crying out for truth and justice."

In his memory, the temple library was renamed the Rabbi Dudley Weinberg Library and a special fund was established to underwrite an annual Scholar in Residence weekend. Each year a noted scholar was engaged to lecture and conduct study sessions throughout a weekend.

Officers and directors of the original Temple Brotherhood. Formed as the Temple Men's Club, the organization's first leaders were directors (standing l-r) Nathan Boruszak, Marvin Fein, Herman Levitz, Samuel Saffro, (seated l-r) Melvin Marshall, president; Marvin Hersh, treasurer; Allen Polacheck, secretary; and Charles Goldberg, vice-president. Not shown are Clarence Jung, Samuel E. Kohn and Adolph Mandelker. Although this original board was elected in 1933, this photograph was taken in 1973 when the men were honored in a Sabbath service celebrating the Brotherhood's 40th anniversary.

Rabbi Barry Silberg

Scholars who conducted seminars and sermons in these events included Dr. Abraham Sachar, founding president of Brandeis University; the well-known Orthodox rabbi, Dr. Irving Greenberg; Rabbi Gunther Plaut of Toronto's huge Holy Blossom Temple; Roland Gittleson, Rabbi Emeritus of Boston's Temple Israel and Dr. Ezra Spicehandler.

Rabbi Weinberg's death left the Board of Trustees to resolve a knotty problem of succession. Young Rabbi Silberg had joined the staff as associate just two years earlier from his position in Roanoke, Virginia. He lacked the official years of experience normally required by the Central Conference of American Rabbis to lead a congregation

Dance Service
For A
Friday Evening

Experimental services became part of the worship experience in the mid-twentieth century. Rabbi Silberg commissioned this local dance group to create an entire service conducted in dance and it was performed on a Friday night in 1978. Music on which the program was based had been written by a cantor in New York and was considered particularly appropriate for such a service.

of 1,400 families, but his flamboyant style, engaging personality, incisive preaching and superior scholarship belied his lack of experience and won the enthusiastic support of the members. Congregation leaders sensed that if a new Senior Rabbi was appointed, Rabbi Silberg would accept a large pulpit of his own as soon as he was officially qualified. Not wanting to lose so dynamic a leader, the Board elected to retain him as Senior Rabbi in spite of the customary rules. The move was to cast a die that would shape the congregation for the next 23 years.

THE MILWAUKEE JOURNAL   Thursday, November 16, 1978

Synagog Set for 1st Look at Dancers

By Paula Goldman
of The Journal Staff

Through the doors and down the aisles they marched to the front of the synagog, their hands held high. In a swirling circle the young women danced, rejoicing for the joy of the Lord.

Members of Dance Offering, a liturgical modern dance troupe, were rehearsing for the performance of a complete Friday evening service scheduled for 8:15 p.m. Dec. 1 at Temple Emanuel, 2419 E. Kenwood Blvd.

Although Dance Offering has appeared in area churches, it is the troupe's first appearance in a synagog. It is also the first time, according to Rabbi Barry Silberg, that a Milwaukee area synagog will have a complete service in dance.

The troupe is headed by Pamela Frautschi, who has the Dance Spectrum studio at 3555 N. Oakland Ave., Shorewood. It was commissioned last spring by Silberg to create a work to accompany David Benedict's "A Dance Service for Friday Eve."

Benedict is a cantor at a temple on Long Island and a professor of music at Adelphi University.

Part of Jewish Spirit

Temple Emanuel cantor Donald Roberts said:
"Movement has always been part of the Jewish spirit. Miriam danced before the waters of the Red Sea, and there's always dancing at the end of a wedding in the Hasidic sect."

Hasidim is an Orthodox sect combining emotional aspects with intellectualism in practicing Judaism.

Roberts referred to "shukling" or rhythmic movement during "davaning" or prayer as an antecedent of dance. It is a rocking motion of the upper part of the body.

"This is a service," he said. "We're using dance as a form of interpreting liturgy. She (Ms. Frautschi) has studied every word, not just the idea, used in the service.

"Art and music have no politics."

40 Minute Dance

The dance will take 40 minutes of the 1 hour, 20 minute service.

"This is quite liberal," Roberts said. "It could possibly offend some of the congregation. We've had sermon presentations with dance. I don't know how a whole service will go over.

"Dance has to be experienced. And movement has to be brought back to the service. Movement can interpret liturgy the same way art can. Words are not always the best medium."

Silberg said:
"Dance is an intimate part of Jewish prayer. The congregation prays in Hebrew and English. Dance is an affiliate. If it is done with skill, it is no less appropriate than cantorial song. Some will no doubt find it inspiring, distracting, amusing. If the performance achieves

Turn to Troupe, page 8, col. 5

Troupe
Synagog Ready for Dancers

From Page 1

its ends, it will elicit a spiritual response which cannot be guaranteed."

The religious experience shouldn't be exclusively cerebral.

"Sexual intimacies are a presumption that has more to do with the perceiver than the dancers. Some might find it offensive."

Not a Gimmick

Silberg said dancing was not a gimmick to get people to attend services. There is everything to gain from this experience and almost nothing to lose, he said. The worst that could happen is that too few people will be reached, he said.

The dancers are getting into form not only by extensive rehearsing, but also by listening to lectures on Jewish thought given by Silberg and members of the Hebrew school staff.

Dance is another way of communicating the message of prayer, Ms. Frautschi said.
"If you say the Pledge of Allegiance to the flag every day, you don't think about it," she said. "It no longer has any meaning."

Dance is a way of renewing awareness, she said, and dancing in a synagog presents new challenges to the dancers. As choreographer, Ms. Frautschi had to be careful not to use stereotypical Christian gestures such as the sign of the cross.

More Open Space

The synagog is easier to dance in than a typical church, she said. For one thing there are no communion rails or choirs as structural barriers, and there is more open space on the pulpit.

In her choreography Ms. Frautschi applies the universals of dance to the universals of religion, she said.
"Dancing is as appropriate in a temple as in any church," she said. "There is nothing in the dance that doesn't fall into the universal. We are always up against dancing in a church as a sacrilege. But it is an expression, like singing."

Members of Dance Offering rehearsed the 'Benediction Dance' at Temple Emanuel
—Journal Photo by Donald W. Nusbaum

Rabbi Silberg soon acted with boundless energy and a swift hand. He acted forcefully in the area of Jewish education, supporting the new, less formal teaching techniques of Educational Director Michael Fefferman, who had been recruited by Rabbi Weinberg. Fefferman added a bold camping program to be integrated with creative, new concepts instituted in Religious School classroom studies. He introduced trope (Hebrew chanting) to the

Hebrew school training. The success of the program was due, according to Fefferman, to the establishment of a general Religious School program that was neither Reform, Conservative, nor Orthodox. "We also dealt with many secular problems such as the 'age-old' tradition of students 'sneaking out' of classes" to the frequented oasis of nearby Riegleman's Drugstore. Michael Fefferman put an abrupt halt to his truant students when he shocked them with his own surprise appearance at Reigleman's.

Rabbi Silberg, working together with congregants Phillip Rubinstein and Doris Schneidman, played a key role in the development of the Milwaukee Jewish Day School. The school opened in September, 1981 with 11 students and three teachers, finally fulfilling a wish of the late Rabbi Weinberg. Providing a respectful environment for all streams of Judaism, the school "lived" at the synagogue for the first three years of its existence. An expanded, educationally vital school was then able to move into its own quarters on Santa Monica Blvd. in Whitefish Bay, where it has continued to provide quality Jewish education for an ever increasing number of students.

Rabbi Barry Silberg
1976

Having lost part of the land to city road construction and without a burial since 1888, Hopkins Street Cemetery had fallen into disrepair. Aged and damaged monuments were removed and a new single monument containing the names of those interred was dedicated.

Well known in the community outside the congregation, Rabbi Silberg was an outspoken advocate for civil rights, and human justice and a proponent of handgun control legislation. He served on Mayor Henry Maier's advisory Commission on Human Rights formed after the controversial death of Ernest Lacy, a young black man who died in police custody.

In 1983, he instituted a sanctuary program to protect Latin American political refugees from unwarranted arrest as illegal aliens in the United States. The Ruiz family from El Salvador, seeking political asylum in the United States, was the first to live in the synagogue building after the Board overcame objections of a congregational minority that feared the activity would be an illegal act by the congregation and would expose it to considerable liability. Others from Afghanistan and Guatamala arrived later. While no other Jewish congregation in the United States had instituted such a program, Catholic and Protestant churches had done so.

Rabbi Silberg was also co-chairman of a statewide inter-religious organization for a moratorium on nuclear war. Cognizant of the growing friction between African-American and Jewish communities locally as well as nationally, he instituted a pulpit exchange with the inner city Mount Zion Baptist Church.

Recognizing the need to accommodate Christian-born people desiring to adopt the Jewish religion, Rabbi Silberg turned to the scholarly, respected Dr. Herman Weil to design and conduct a program of instruction, which they called Adult Confirmation for potential converts. Students in the intensive program were required to meet regularly with Dr. Weil and Rabbi Silberg, attend services, learn Hebrew and write a 10-page term paper before qualifying for conversion. In a four-year period, 50 candidates completed the course to become Jews by Choice.

Dr. Herman Weil

A scholar of distinguished background, Dr. Weil turned to Emanu-El B'ne Jeshurun

Weddings are among the most cherished uses of the synagogue. They gather friends and families together from remote locations for one of the happiest of occasions. This Kenwood Blvd. ceremony united Steven Gruen and Mardee Stern in 1968.

almost immediately on his arrival from Germany. Having been stripped of both his professorship and his high academic credentials by the Nazis, he was confined at Buchenwald concentration camp. Released from confinement in 1938, he found his way to the United States and joined the staff of (now) University of Wisconsin-Milwaukee, ultimately rising to the level of Assistant Provost. He began his service to Emanu-El B'ne Jeshurun as a part time Religious School Director and retained the position until the appointment of a full time director in the late 1940's.

Having served Rabbis Baron, Weinberg and Silberg, he led worship services in their absence, conducted funeral services on an emergency basis, and performed a lifetime

63

Refugees Find Sanctuary in Milwaukee Synagogue

Refugees seeking political asylum in the U.S. at Congregation Emanu-El B'ne Jeshurun of Milwaukee. From left to right: Qudsia Baka (Afghanistan), Rabbi Francis Barry Silberg, Juanita (El Salvador), and Jorge (Guatemala).

Joined by Holocaust survivors, Soviet immigrants, and several masked Latin American refugees, Rabbi Francis Barry Silberg declared from the pulpit of Congregation Emanu-El B'ne Jeshurun of Milwaukee, "Thou shalt not stand idle while thy neighbor bleeds," initiating his congregation's sanctuary program for refugees of oppression seeking political asylum in the U.S. The synagogue, which has fought for years to preserve and extend civil liberties and civil rights in Milwaukee and the Midwest, is the first in America to embark upon this type of program. Roman Catholic and Protestant churches in Milwaukee and elsewhere have pioneered in such sanctuary efforts.

After its Sabbath of Conscience last April, Rabbi Silberg announced that the Ruiz family of El Salvador, which was formally requested political asylum in the U.S., would be the first refugees to be supported by the synagogue. Silberg also made public the congregation's plans to aid Quadsia Baka of Afghanistan, who believes that if she returns to her homeland she will be shot for speaking out against the Soviets during a university rally.

Comparing the plight of the Latin American refugees to European Jews during the Holocaust seeking a safe haven in vain, Rabbi Silberg first introduced this idea in a sermon delivered on December 3, 1982. He appealed to the congregants to begin assisting and providing sanctuary to Latin American refugees. The matter was referred to the congregation's Social Action Committee, headed by James Zucker, which began studying the issue in detail.

After two months, the committee delivered a proposal for Board consideration. Despite concern by a minority of group members that harboring these aliens would be illegal and subject temple leaders to arrest and possible conviction, the committee nevertheless recommended to the Board that all persons fleeing oppression, including illegal aliens, be offered sanctuary.

The Board later sided with the minority opinion of the Social Action Committee, which preferred to harbor in the synagogue only those persons seeking political asylum. In addition, the resolution passed by the Board committed the synagogue to an intensive lobbying campaign to change U.S. policy toward individuals fleeing from El Salvador and Guatemala, pledged material and finan-cial aid to organizations helping refugees from Latin America, offered counseling for illegal aliens, and agreed to create a legal defense fund to support those pursuing asylum.

The congregation, in providing refugees with counseling and legal defense funds, provides those seeking asylum with more than sanctuary. Says Rabbi Silberg, "We are seeking to do the greatest good for the greatest number of people by offering "not only a safe haven but a community." He sees the program as a model that can be used by synagogues across America and says, "Just think, what if every synagogue adopted one family? Twenty-five hundred families, one hundred thousand people. What a statement that would make!"

of valuable educational activities, which continued unbroken until his death in 1998. For his years of dedicated service culminating in the Adult Confirmation Program, the congregation designated him a Distinguished Service Fellow.

Particular note must also be given to Lillian Friedman's lifelong service to the synagogue. Miss Friedman came to

Rabbi Silberg unveiled the plaque mounted on the wall of Milwaukee County Courthouse in 1984 identifying the location of the original B'ne Jeshurun as the area's first synagogue.

Emanu-El B'ne Jeshurun as Rabbi Baron's secretary. Seven years later, she became the first Executive Secretary. For 45 years, she handled every detail connected with synagogue administration including High Holiday seat assignments in the 1940's, member communications, dues collection, bulletin preparation, expense and payment controls and a multitude of tasks assigned by the rabbis or requested from members.

Program distributed to attendants at the dedication of a plaque marking the site of the original building of B'ne Jeshurun on the present County Courthouse location. The program was signed by some of those attending the ceremony. Many were descendants of the original B'ne Jeshurun members.

Always thinking of ways to enhance and promote the synagogue, Miss Friedman initiated the idea of the bronze plaque that since 1984 has graced the Wells St. entrance to the Milwaukee County Courthouse. She organized a dedication ceremony attended by County Executive William O'Donnell and other government officials as well as present generations of the original B'ne Jeshurun families. Rabbi Silberg unveiled the plaque, which reads:

66

"Upon this site stood B'ne Jeshurun synagogue,
the first Jewish congregation in Milwaukee County.
Dedicated September 27, 1886 Razed March, 1928
before the construction of the Milwaukee County
Courthouse"

In May, 1996 Miss Friedman conceived the idea of an educational open house for non-Jews, offering them a chance to learn more about Jews and Judaism. She recruited Board members as docents to lead tours during an afternoon that was advertised as "A Visit to Milwaukee's Oldest Synagogue". Over 200 people attended the event.

On retirement in 1979, she was appointed congregational Archivist and organized a valuable repository of the documents, manuscripts, letters, minute books, photographs, and bound volumes of weekly/monthly bulletins dating from the acquisition of land for the original B'ne Jeshurun temple in 1856. The complete archives are now housed in the Milwaukee Jewish Historical Society. She later spearheaded a drive for an in-house display of memorabilia selected from this collection called the Gallery of Congregational History. This display, originally hung in the Kenwood Blvd. building, has been rehung on the Vera and Joseph Zilber Campus in River Hills.

A living repository of congregational history, Miss Friedman was honored on her 85th birthday when the Temple Archives was renamed the "Lillian Friedman

The 125th anniversary in 1981 was a grand celebration that extended beyond the temple family. The event was honored by this commemorative, lighted sign on the face of City Hall.

Archives," where she continued to serve as Archivist until her death in 1998.

"Her soul, her very being was immersed in the life, the joys, the sorrows of this congregation," Rabbi Silberg eulogized at her funeral. "Lillian graced the place, breathed, ate and slept the place. She taught us to go the extra mile, make the extra effort, send the right message, do the right thing."

By 1981 the congregation reached the stately age of 125 years and a year-long celebration was launched with

The event drew a capacity crowd to the Hotel Pfister Ballroom where Rabbi Alexander Schindler, president of UAHC was the featured speaker.

a Founders' Day Shabbat using a liturgy assembled from elements taken from all the different prayer books used since 1856. One year in the planning, the celebration was chaired by Ben and Mimi Chernov. A full calendar of religious, educational, cultural and social events were on the agenda including historical displays, a Milwaukee Art Museum exhibition of liturgical silver objects from the Joseph Baron Museum collection and the creation of an original work of art by photo-artist Arnold Gore depicting the anniversary

69

theme, "Our Inherited Future." A culminating banquet at the Hotel Pfister completed the celebration.

Spurred by the 125th anniversary year, a number of diverse and creative programs emerged from a program services committee. They provided a multitude of occasions for members and non-members alike to come to the synagogue for non-worship activities and to find a place for it in their lives. A Young Mothers' Support Group, transportation to Sabbath services for the elderly and infirm, an Alcoholics Anonymous group were just a sampling of a broad spectrum of special services.

Rabbi Silberg and Cantor Eichaker conduct a service in the picturesque chapel added to the Kenwood building in 1983. Colorful stained glass windows in the background represent the 12 tribes of Israel. Produced by Conrad-Schmitt Studios of Milwaukee in conjunction with design consultation by Rabbi Silberg. Furniture and interior design are of the Classical European style. Pulpit chairs are copies of those from Touro Synagogue in Newport, R.I., America's first synagogue.

Continuing the "community house" concept initiated
by Rabbi Weinberg, Rabbi Silberg used the synagogue
as a venue for many cultural and social events including
a piano concert by Milwaukee Symphony Orchestra
conductor Lucas Foss, and lectures by Jewish genealogist
Arthur Kurzweill and then-Jerusalem Post reporter Wolf
Blitzer. Other special evenings were A Night of Yiddish, a
program of Klezmer music, and a 50-year reunion for the
Confirmation Class of 1933.

Until 1984 the sanctuary was the sole venue for worship
services. A 250-seat chapel had been on the "want list" for
over a decade, but fundraising for the 1975 expansion had
not been sufficient for its inclusion. Unsatisfied with the
absence of the chapel, the Temple Brotherhood spearheaded
a campaign headed by Jacob Beck and Joe Smith to raise the
necessary funds and a spectacular chapel was completed late
in 1983. Against a contemporary background of colorful,
artistic windows, the room was designed in the style of an
18th century synagogue. The ark was a replica of a world
famous ark crafted in 1770 in Weilheim, Germany. The
sexton's bench and chairs were replicas of those in Touro
Synagogue of Newport, RI.

Heading Toward the 21st Century

By the mid-1980's the effect of Jewish population movement ever farther from Kenwood Blvd. into the northern suburbs became increasingly painful. More and more families were reluctant to transport pre-teenage children to late afternoon Hebrew school, even on a school bus. Members became attracted to other, more

Exterior of the merged Congregation Emanu-El B'ne Jeshurun on Kenwood Blvd., home from 1923 to 1997. A large addition of classrooms and badly needed office space was constructed in 1974 and an unusual chapel was completed nine years later.

conveniently located, synagogues--Congregation Sinai and
Congregation Shalom, both spawned in earlier decades
from Emanu-El B'ne Jeshurun. Having sold the large tract
of Fox Point land after the decision to expand in the city,
the lack of an alternate site was becoming an irritating
problem.

Despite the lack of any specific plan to relocate, a
search for an appropriate suburban site went on for years
until a 10-acre parcel of land became available on Brown
Deer Rd. in the Village of River Hills. It was purchased
in December, 1995 with idea of constructing a building to
serve primarily as a Religious School and meeting center
with a chapel of limited size. Trustees believed that the
facility would attract new families with school-age children
and the resulting revenue increase would make it feasible to
operate both the main building in the city and the satellite
in River Hills.

Only after protracted negotiations and contentious
public hearings did village officials grant approval for the
project, even then rejecting the proposed exterior design and
requiring that it match the colonial character of surrounding
buildings.

Groundbreaking finally took place in the fall of 1996. A
year later, the red brick colonial satellite venue was opened.
It was named the Joseph and Vera Zilber Campus in honor
of the major donors to the project.

Reform Jews Buy a Tract

20 Acres in River Hills Acquired for Future Congregation Needs

Congregation Emanu-El B'ne Jeshurun, Milwaukee's largest Reform Jewish congregation, has bought 20 acres of land in River Hills "to meet the needs of the congregation of the long term future."

The property is on the northeast corner of the relocated highway 141 and W. Bradley rd. It was bought from Irving Seaman for an indicated price of $50,000, according to revenue stamps attached to the deed, which was recorded with the register of deeds Friday.

The property has a 500 foot frontage on W. Bradley rd. and a depth of almost 1,800 feet. It includes a house at 480 W. Bradley rd. presently occupied by a Seaman employe.

"Many Years Ahead"

Members of Congregation Emanu-El B'ne Jeshurun have their present synagogue at 2419 E. Kenwood blvd.

In a letter to members of the congregation, Edward R. Prince, president, explained that the officers in approving the purchase were looking "many years ahead."

"Urban living has c h a n g e d drastically in recent years, with the almost explosive movement of people to the suburbs and the fantastic increase in the use of the automobile with all the resulting problems of parking and traffic," Prince said.

Approval Is Unanimous

"Your board of trustees has felt for several years that prudence dictates that the congregation protect its long term future by acquiring acreage in the northeast sector of the city to meet the almost certain continuation of these trends. The center of population of our congregation is already in the southern part of Whitefish Bay.

"Land in the form of acreage, with the possibility of zoning for institutional use, has become almost impossible to find in the highly restricted residential areas of our northern suburbs. And such land must not only have reasonable z o n i n g possibilities but factors of character of surrounding area, proper size, future availability of sewer and public transportation, proximity to the future residence of our membership and reasonable cost are equally important.

"I am happy to report that we have found such land and purchased it after unanimous approval of the board of trustees."

The entire village of River Hills now is zoned for single family residences, J o h n Frederickson, village manager, s a i d Saturday.

Must Apply for Permit

He said that any group planning to erect a church or synagogue would have to apply to the board of appeals, which has the discretion of granting a permit if other requirements including sanitation, setback and building regulations are met.

Buildings covered in this section of the code include schools, churches, public buildings, telephone exchanges, nonprofit clubs and certain temporary structures.

Frederickson said members of the temple had indicated that it might be 10 to 30 years before they would build.

As insurance in the event of a future move to the suburbs, the Board of Trustees purchased a tract of land originally in River Hills, later annexed to Fox Point. The land was sold when the decision was made to expand the Kenwood Blvd. facility in 1974.

For the dedication, members marched in a grand parade for the 10-mile route from Kenwood to Brown Deer Rd. On a beautiful, sun-splashed Sunday, they took turns at the honors of bearing the Torah or carrying the traditional *chuppah* held high above the Torah scrolls. Many walked alongside, happy to be a part of this rare, traditional and meaningful event.

The temple on Kenwood, a stately structure built in 1927 remained the congregation's main location, housing the rabbinical study, sanctuary community hall and business offices as well as the Weinberg Library and schoolrooms. Religious and Hebrew school classes were split between both locations. A schedule of Sabbath services was held on the Zilber Campus as well as at Kenwood.

Two buildings, however, meant double operating costs. It was not long before financial deficits began to mount to uncomfortable levels. Not only were maintenance costs unusually high, but the old building was badly in need of extensive and costly repairs that could not be completed from dues revenue. It became apparent that operating two facilities was beyond the congregation's capability.

Concurrently, the adjacent University of Wisconsin-Milwaukee's Fine Arts Department was experiencing overcrowded conditions in its building across the street and in need of additional performance, rehearsal and office space. UW-M faculty and staff toured the Kenwood building and found it adaptable for their purposes. The university made an offer to purchase. The congregation eventually accepted the offer with contingencies that included the right to hold High Holy Day services there at no charge until 2004. In subsequent years the congregation could rent its former sanctuary at a stipulated rate. Terms of the sale also guaranteed the right to remove stained glass windows from the sanctuary and chapel. Removing the sanctuary windows designed by Rabbi Baron proved to be a risky undertaking. Experts feared that the fragile stained glass, untouched in its frame for nearly 70 years could not survive the move. In addition, the cost of moving and installing would have been prohibitive. The possibility of reusing the windows from the chapel remains a possibility. The Board of Trustees did negotiate agreement that the congregation would retain ownership of the Baron windows, which would remain in their original site on long-term loan to the university.

Not everyone, however, accepted the sale. A dissident group fought tenaciously against the loss of the building, circularizing the membership with a series of angry charges,

The present building on Brown Deer Rd. was originally conceived as a satellite to Kenwood Blvd. primarily as an educational facility, but now functions as the congregation's sole home.

finally filing a personal lawsuit against the officers and trustees. Ultimately, the court dismissed the suit, but not before it cost the congregation and its officers many thousands of dollars in legal fees, the loss of many members and a measure of prestige that was nearly a century and a half in building. The spiteful dissidents had dealt a crippling blow.

Change, it seems, was the order of the day. In 1999, Rabbi Francis Barry Silberg announced his retirement to emeritus status after 22 years as Senior Rabbi of Emanu-El B'ne Jeshurun.

His successor would be Rabbi Marc Berkson of Temple Judea Mizpah in Skokie, Illinois. He had been ordained by the Hebrew Union College-Jewish Institute of Religion in

1978. He had served as president of the Chicago Association of Reform Rabbis and later held the same position with the Wisconsin Council of Rabbis.

"I wanted to come to Emanu-El B'ne Jeshurun," said Rabbi Berkson, "because it was an historic congregation that had encountered difficult times. It presented an opportunity to build a new kind of Reform Judaism.

Rabbi Marc E. Berkson

Acknowledging that all change is difficult, especially in
a religious context, Rabbi Berkson worked tirelessly to build
that new kind of Reform Judaism. Change came first in
the area of music through the collaborative efforts of the
rabbi and Cantor David Barash, who joined the staff in
2001. They introduced an upbeat style of liturgical music
that encouraged worshipers to sing along with the cantor,
who employs a small middle eastern drum called a dumbek
to keep the beat. The congregation shifted rather easily
from the non-involvement seen in most congregations to
an enthusiastic participation in the service. "We have a
wonderful Friday night service with much *ruach* (spirit),"
the cantor said.

L-R: Joe Aaron, Guy
Fiorentini, Cantor David
Barash, Ed Doemland, Ari
David Rosenthal, Mark "Lil
Rev" Revenson

Change has been slower in High Holiday worship
according to Cantor Barash. "It is inspiring to be in that
wonderful Kenwood space and to work with the choir.
There is not as much congregational singing, but then it is a
time of more introspection and active listening."

A more startling variation in the worship experience
instituted by the rabbi and cantor is a service known as
Torahpalooza. Designed to reach out to a youthful audience
not accustomed to frequent temple attendance, it employs
a variety of musical instruments including flute, clarinet,
saxophone, guitar, ukulele and keyboard. The ambience is
not one of traditional reverence, but of enthusiastic singing
and dancing in the aisles followed by an *Oneg Shabbat*
(reception) with wine and beer. While planned as a means

of reaching out to young people, the service increasingly
attracted an older—even senior citizen—following despite
its radical departure from the normal liturgical style.

Building on the success of Torahpalooza, an innovation
for the youngest children was an all-musical, tot-friendly
version. Totpalooza was promoted as "Shabbos with a
Smile" and a dinner for the youngest set and their parents.

Recognizing that a generation of Reform Jewish parents
was raised at Emanu-El B'ne Jeshurun with no training in
Hebrew, Rabbi Berkson instituted an intensive adult study
program called Anshe Mitzvah,
the adult equivalent of Bar
Mitzvah. At the conclusion
of the two years of study, the
program culminates in a group
Bar Mitzvah ceremony.

Commitments to social
justice and to outreach have
inspired Rabbi Berkson's
leadership of the Tikkun Ha-Ir
(Healing of the City) group that
works with other synagogues
and Jewish organizations
and which he regards as an
extension of the temple's historic
connection to the city. Studying

Social Action committee activities
frequently involve joint efforts
with other Jewish, Christian, or
non-sectarian groups. Tikkun
Ha-Ir, a multi-congregational
group involving Emanu-El B'ne
Jeshurun, is shown in a project
to collect clothing and household
items for use in homeless shelters
and recovery programs.

biblical texts applicable to each of its projects, Tikkun Ha-Ir volunteers serve meals to the hungry and staff city shelters for the homeless.

Having reached his 25th year in the rabbinate in 2006, Marc Berkson was awarded an honorary Doctor of Divinity degree from the Hebrew Union College-Jewish Institute of Religion. The congregation honored him with a special service featuring "Yachad, a Travelling Tefillah Band" and a personal favorite of the rabbi's. The occasion also marked the initiation of a Torah Restoration Fund for costly and arduous task of repairing the worn parchment and lettering in the congregation's only restorable Torah scroll.

The 150th Anniversay year of 2006 brought a round of celebratory events beginning with a congregational tour of Israel led by Rabbi Berkson. A city-wide theater performance featuring Craig Taubman, widely-known musician and composer whose songs meld traditional Jewish themes with contemporary Jewish life, was held at the Riverside Theater. Taubman's lively, invigorating style breathes new life into religious services in appearances throughout the country including one in Washington D.C. at the White House.

To commemorate its sesquicentennial, the congregation commissioned Taubman to compose a special song. His "Lo Alecha" (The Time is Short and There's Much Work to Be Done) was premiered at the Riverside concert. In a service similar to that by Rabbi Silberg at the 125th anniversary utilizing all the Reform prayerbooks of previous years, Rabbi Berkson led a Saturday morning Heritage Shabbat service employing the widely recognized Union Prayer Book that preceded the present Gates of Prayer introduced in 1975.

"Lettering Our Legacy" was a sesquicentennial event that continued during the year. The commissioning of a new Torah brought the scribe who would supervise the lettering to Milwaukee, where young and old were accorded the privilege of actually writing a letter onto the parchment. The opening ceremony kept the scribe busy throughout a Sunday afternoon guiding the hands of those who performed the mitzvah of writing in a new Torah. In addition to contributions by those who participated in the hands-on writing, sponsorships were available not only for one letter, but one word, one of the five books, one of the weekly Torah portions or for the

In commemoration of the 150th anniversary, the congregation commissioned an original musical composition, *Lo Alecha* (Time is Short and There's Much Work to Be Done), by Craig Laubman. Earlier a commission created the music for the Shalom R'av (Grant Us Peace) prayer commony used by congregations throughout the country.

Still underway at the 150th year is the Lettering Our Legacy project in which members and their children and grandchildren have the opportunity to enter a single letter into a Torah that will find its home in the Brown Deer Rd. ark. Under the supervision of Rabbi Moshe Druin, President Sandra Kohler Stern is entering a letter surrounded by husband Scott Stern, Rabbi Berkson and Cantor Barasch.

breastplate, crown or rollers adorning the Torah itself. Donations from the project were earmarked for rebuilding the Endowment Fund, which had been severely deminished by operating losses of recent years.

Other sesquicentennial events were a Brotherhood Sports Night featuring temple member and Baseball Commissioner Allan H. (Bud) Selig, and a Rededication Ceremony of the Hopkins St. Cemetery, which was the first religious act performed by the new Jewish community in 1847.

As happened on nearly every milestone anniversary year, a celebratory banquet was held at Milwaukee Hilton Hotel with Doris Kearns Goodwin, nationally renown historian and author as featured speaker.

Pillars of the Synagogue

The two vital support arms of the temple are Women of Reform Judaism and the Brotherhood. The members of both groups have volunteered their services to do just about every task needed to keep the congregation operating smoothly—from fund raising to Purim carnivals; From sukka decorating to running an annual Blood Bank.

Women of Reform Judaism had a forerunner in the 19th century. The Emanu-El Ladies Society, organized in 1872, was dedicated to raising money for the temple's treasury primarily through concerts, New Year's dances, Purim and Simchat Torah balls. The group functioned under this name until 1919 when it became Emanu-El Sisterhood. Its Articles of Organization stated its purposes to be "promotion of the works and interests of the congregation and the cultivation of the religious spirit by assisting in the Religious School". These purposes were to be accomplished by "meetings, lectures and pursuits of intellectual, social and instructional means."

Talent shows and musical reviews were often produced, usually by the Brotherhood or Sisterhood and almost always to rave reviews. This 1959 version was one of many successes.

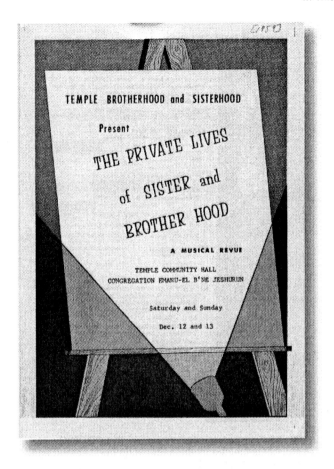

So strong was the similar group at B'ne Jeshurun that it cast a unanimous vote of over 300 members protesting the Board's acceptance of Rabbi Levi's resignation in 1926 and insisted on a vote of the full congregation. The Board rejected the plea, but the women made their presence felt.

By 1931, two years after the merger of Emanu-El and B'ne Jeshurun, the Sisterhood membership had grown to 546.

Circa 1950, Louise Abrahams Yaffe, a mother of three young children, became president and revitalized the group by introducing a circle system. Circles were interest groups that chose their own meeting times, social events and fundraising projects. The circles remained active for six to eight years. During this era, two members of Sisterhood, Yaffe and Dori Chortek served on the board of the National Federation of Temple Sisterhoods.

In the mid-twentieth century years, Sisterhood became very active. For several years an Antiques Show was the primary fundraising effort. Other projects included an interfaiath educational outreach to non-Jewish women called "We Speak for Judaism."

Brotherhood President Robert W. Kohn receives 1968-69 Program Award from fellow-congregant and national Brotherhood board member Mel Sinykin.

Sisterhood also participated in Services to the Sightless, recruiting volunteers to tape record textbooks for the blind or partially sighted students.

Other notable activities were an annual American Field Service Sabbath when members invited foreign exchange students for a home Sabbath dinner and Friday night service. Sisterhood also administered the sale of Uniongrams, messages sent for happy or sad occasions that raised funds for their myriad projects.

The end of the century brought important societal changes that slowed the activity of the Sisterhood under the weight of time-crippling schedules for young family women, a great many of whom also filled jobs outside the home. The change of name to Women of Reform Judaism brought with it a new outlook and a modernized structure of "user-friendly" programs and meeting times designed to harmonize with the contemporary lifestyle.

The Brotherhood was one of the early members of the National Federation of Temple Brotherhoods (NFTB), joining the national group in 1933 just 10 years after its inception. Members who have served on the NFTB board include Mike Frank, Marvin Kohner, Matty Katz, Edward Fine, Maury Goldstein and Mel Sinykin, a national vice-president.

Highlights of the Brotherhood include an annual Institute for Christian Clergy initiated in 1956, which has become one of the projects of the national Jewish Chatauqua Society. In 1969, Brotherhood received the NFTB's top programming award. In 1974, it earned top honors for its publication, the "Brotherhood Columns" newsletter.

Brotherhoods of the three local Reform congregations hosted an NFTB Executive Board meeting in 1975. So successful was that conclave that the Emanu-El B'ne Jeshurun Brotherhood prepared a step-by-step "How To" manual to the hosting of these meetings. The Brotherhood has for many years sponsored a Blood Bank that attracted over 100 donors. Other notable activities were Lox Box sales, serving at church-organized meal programs and

many social and family recreational and sports activities.
The group publishes an annual Calendar\Congregational
Directory, builds and mans a "mobile sukkah" that travels
to members' homes to join sukah parties, and hosts an
annual Deli Dinner. Funds derived from the various events
have supported purchase of many of the temple's needs
including new computer equipment for the temple office
and funded scholarships for congregational youth through
its Fefferman Campership Fund.

Fundraising projects by the Brotherhood and Sisterhood raised money for many important projects such as the Brotherhood's leadership contribution to the Chapel Fund in 1984. The annual sale of a Sunday Breakfast "Lox Box" has been a consistent success for many years.

The contemporary Brotherhood today remains highly
active and dedicated to serving Emanu-El B'ne Jeshurun as
it has for over 70 years.

Looking Back

There are striking differences between Jewish life in Milwaukee's pioneer days of the 1850's and the fast, computer-generated pace of the 21st century. In 2006, Emanu-El B'ne Jeshurun practices Reform Judaism, but its antecedents used the Orthodox *minhag* (worship style) brought to the United States by German Jews.

In the middle of the 19th century a small knot of immigrants observed Yom Kippur together in a rented room above a grocery store. In 2006, many hundreds of congregants gather for High Holy Day services.

In the 1850's, the early rabbis were natives of European countries. They were educated and ordained in European yeshivas and they preferred to preach in German. In the past century, the rabbis have been American-born and educated at the Reform Jewish seminary, Hebrew Union College-Jewish Institute of Religion with campuses in New York, Los Angeles and Jerusalem as well as the original Cincinnati location.

In the beginning, congregations conducted all meetings and business in German, the native language of the founders. Now everything is in English and sermons in German are a part of the quaint and distant past.

In sanctuaries of the 1850's women were relegated to balcony seating during services and did not participate in business meetings. In the present, Reform women function as true equals with men, acting as Torah bearers and readers, Board of Trustees members and committee chairs. In its 150th year, Emanu-El B'ne Jeshurun is, for the fourth time, served by a woman president.

At age 150, Congregation Emanu-El B'ne Jeshurun looks proudly to its past. The moral leadership of its rabbis has been a strong force in metropolitan affairs as well as those of the Jewish community. Its early presidents and board members were also founding members of the Milwaukee Jewish Council for Community Relations, Jewish Family Services and Federated Jewish Charities (now Milwaukee Jewish Federation). Lizzie Kander (Mrs. Simon), a synagogue member in the 1920's and 1930's was one of the first in Milwaukee to perform social work on behalf of Russian immigrants who flooded into the city in the 1880's. She founded the Milwaukee Jewish Mission, using the borrowed quarters of Temple B'ne Jeshurun and Temple Emanu-El. She was an early worker for the Jewish Settlement House (now Jewish Community Center) and

her still famous Settlement Cook Book was a
substantial source of income for the JCC.

In the long journey of Congregation
Emanu-El B'ne Jeshurun to its
sesquicentennial year, the road has
not always been smooth. Along
the way there have been mergers,
dissident members, split-offs to
form other congregations, changes
of rabbis, cantors and educational
directors and changes of address
while relocating in downtown
Milwaukee, moving to the East Side
and most recently to it's suburban River
Hills location.

At 150 years old, Congregation Emanu-El B'ne
Jeshurun is a historic congregation that continues to grow
as it emerges into the ever-changing Reform Judaism of the
21st century and beyond.

An undated
photograph of Simon
and Lizzie Black Kander.

Looking Ahead

What will Reform Judaism be like for the upcoming generation? Change is on its way according to Rabbi Berkson, who is leading the congregation forward in the 21st century. "It happens with each generation, approximately once every 25-40 years," he observed. Historically, each generation has needed to find its own definition of what it means to be a Jew and what they must do to be Jewish.

"The immigrant generation felt a sense of security in the Jewish neighborhoods," the rabbi said. "Their sons and daughters knew the togetherness of close family relationships, but the next generation is becoming scattered about the country in search of more exciting locations offering greater career opportunity. They need to attach to a new 'extended family' and the synagogue must be prepared to fill that role."

To ease the task, Rabbi Berkson sees a gradual blurring of the lines dividing Orthodox, Conservative and Reform factions. These labels will mean little in the future. Some geographical areas might not even have all three represented in convenient locations. Today's young people are far better educated than their parents and grandparents. They are equipped with improved Hebrew skills, and knowledge of Jewish history and bible. Nourished by the strong impact of the State of Israel, more intensive religious school, day school and camping experiences have caused a narrowing of factional identity. "Fewer differences exist and the younger generation going forth from Emanu-El B'ne Jeshurun can feel comfortable in nearly any congregation," he said.

The worship experience will be far less formal in the new century. Recent synagogue architecture has lowered the *bima* and surrounded it with seating, rejecting the theater\ stage orientation. "The rabbi wants to be a part of the congregation, not apart from it," Berkson explained. The rabbi and congregants will worship together as one and not "perform" separate roles.

Changes in the society that see both spouses employed outside the home and chasing tight schedules with their families will result in more frequent observance in the home and increased importance of the Saturday morning service.

"Improving socio-economic status customarily is accompanied by a declining birth rate, resulting in an aging population," he indicated "and that is what we are experiencing early in the new century. There will be less of us, increasing the central role the synagogue and congregation must play." Rabbi Berkson is looking forward to the challenge. He has already begun.

Acknowledgements

The manuscript for this history was written during the winter of 2006 far away from the the facts and figures needed to tell the sesquicentennial story of Congregation Emanu-El B'ne Jeshurun. The Milwaukee Jewish Historical Society was an invaluable resource whose archives yielded critical information. Before I could begin to write I spent many hours there studying the interesting events of the last 150 years. During the writing phase, I could always count on the Society's help by phone, fax or e-mail to verify the accuracy of my facts. My special thanks go to Society Director Kathie Bernstein and Archivist Jay Hyland whose knowledge and skills helped pinpoint needed facts and information.

Another important source was "The History of the Jews of Milwaukee" by Rabbi Louis J. Swichkow, published in 1963 by the Jewish Publication Society of America. My thanks to JPS for graciously granting permission to republish the book's lists of rabbis and congregational presidents.

My thanks also to Journal Communications Inc., publishers of the Milwaukee Journal Sentinel and successor to Wisconsin News, and to Reform Judaism magazine for permission to reprint their articles.

Those were the sources of yesteryear. Helpful in assembling data for the modern period were Ben Chernov, president from 1971-74 and five other living past presidents. I am also indebted to Sandra Kohler Stern, current president and the entire staff of the synagogue. Pulling the manuscript and photographs together into an attractive design was congregrant Kat Grinker, graphic designer. Her contribution was essential to the completion of this book. And finally, my husband, Jim, provided inestimable value in the editing and production of the book. His vision for the project, and the knowledge and passion that emerged from his lifelong association with Congregation Emanu-El B'ne Jeshurun.

Ruth Fromstein

March, 2006

RABBIS OF THE CONGREGATION

Congregation B' ne Jeshurun

Rabbi Isidor Kalisch 1857-60

Rabbi Ferdinand Leopold Sarner.......................................1860

Rabbi Samson Falk 1863-66

Rabbi G.M. Cohen 1868

Rabbi Elias Eppstein 1869-80

Rabbi Emanuel Gerechter 1880-92

Rabbi Victor Caro...1892-1911

Rabbi Charles Levi.. 1913-17

Congregation Emanu-El

Rabbi Edward Benj. Morris Browne 1870

Rabbi Moritz Spitz 1872-78

Rabbi Isaac S. Moses 1879-87

Rabbi Sigmund Hecht 1888-99

Rabbi Julius Meyer 1900-04

Rabbi Samuel Hirshberg 1904-47

Congregation Emanu-El B' ne Jeshurun

Rabbi Joseph L. Baron 1926-51

Rabbi Harry Pastor 1947-51

Rabbi Herbert H. Friedman 1951-55

Rabbi Dudley Weinberg 1955-76

Rabbi F. Barry Silberg 1974-99

Rabbi Marc Berkson 2000-

ASSOCIATE &
ASSISTANT RABBIS

Congregation Emanu-El B' ne Jeshurun

Rabbi Murray Salzman 1956-58

Rabbi William Greenebaum.................................... 1959-61

Rabbi William Schenkerman 1961-62

Rabbi Clyde Sills.. 1963-65

Rabbi Chaim Stern 1965-69

Rabbi Stanley Davids 1969-71

Rabbi Frederick Wenger 1971-74

Rabbi F. Barry Silberg 1974-76

Rabbi Steven Kushner 1977-80

Rabbi Ronald Bluming.. 1980-81

Rabbi Allen Tufts.. 1982-88

Rabbi Steven Adams 1984-88

Rabbi Daniel Lipper.. 1988-94

CANTORS

Congregation Emanu-El B' ne Jeshurun

Anthony Scott, Cantor 1951-52

Sol Altschuller, Cantor 1952-64

Roy Garber, Cantor.. 1965-77

Donald Roberts, Cantor... 1977-80

Nancy Hauseman, Cantor...................................... 1980-82

Frances Ginsberg, Cantorial Soloist........................ 1982-83

Ronald Eichaker, Cantor 1983-

David Blumberg, Cantorial Soloist.....................2000-2001

David Barasch, Cantor 2001-

Printed in the United States
63431LVS00003B/37-234

9 781425 974879